GANGSTERS, NARCOTICS, HOMICIDE

Protecting the Thin Blue Line

MAURICE L. LANDRUM

Detective/Sergeant II (Retired)

CONTENTS

CHAPTER 1
Childhood Dreams 1

CHAPTER 2
Back to California 9

CHAPTER 3
Beginning The Process 15

CHAPTER 4
The Los Angeles Police Academy 21

CHAPTER 5
In The Line Of Duty 27

CHAPTER 6
Harbor Community Police Station 37

CHAPTER 7
Graduation Day 45

CHAPTER 8
Police Officer I 49

CHAPTER 9
1984 Summer Olympic Games 67

CHAPTER 10
Pacific Community Police Station 73

CHAPTER 11
Off-Duty Officer-Involved Shooting 79

CHAPTER 12
California Felony Murder Rule 85

CHAPTER 13
West Bureau CRASH 91

CHAPTER 14
Welcome to the Wild Southwest...99

CHAPTER 15
39th Street and Dalton Avenue...115

CHAPTER 16
Drive-by Shooting Team...135

CHAPTER 17
Rodney King Incident...149

CHAPTER 18
South Bureau Homicide...163

CHAPTER 19
Michael Hubert Hughes (Serial Killer)...183

CHAPTER 20
Northeast Community Patrol Station...187

CHAPTER 21
South Bureau Homicide-COMIT...193

CHAPTER 22
Patrolling Watts...199

CHAPTER 23
Northeast Patrol, Second Tour...203

CHAPTER 24
Officer-Involved Shooting...209

CHAPTER 25
Promotion and Retirement...215

PREFACE

This book is about my journey as a Los Angeles Police Officer. It is a tribute to the hardworking men and women of the Los Angeles Police Department (LAPD). This book details my path from childhood to being sworn in as a member of the LAPD.

On May 2, 1983, my journey began as a Recruit Officer in the Los Angeles Police Academy. There were some major obstacles along the way, such as occasional weak leadership, gangsters, violent street crimes, homicides, a narcotics epidemic and city politics.

Many of my non-sworn friends and family have asked me what was it really like to work the streets of Los Angeles during the early eighties? Well for starters; the city of Los Angeles hosted the 23rd Olympic Games. The economy had suffered a major real estate market crash; there was a rock cocaine and PCP epidemic. There was an increase in gang-related homicides throughout the city of Los Angeles and to top it off, the Los Angeles Police Department had been served with a federal consent decree seeking to rectify unfair hiring and promotional practices involving minorities and women.

This book is dedicated to my wife, children, and grandchildren, as well as, to the many, many law enforcement officers past, present, and future. I had the distinct honor and privilege of serving with some of the most talented and well-trained police officers in the world. So, get ready to read along as I offer an inside look at the real LAPD. No lights or cameras, just plain old-fashioned police work.

During my tenure as a Los Angeles Police Officer, my personal enforcement motto and philosophy was a full patrol car was a happy car, specifically

when it came to arresting gangsters, burglars, robbers, thieves, dope dealers, rapist, murders, and domestic violence suspects. During the eighties, we were Violent Men for Violent Times, and so were the gangsters!

Patrol-Ready

LAPD Class, May 1983

LAPD Recruit Class of May 1983

Kathy Age	Michael D. Johnson	Gerry L. Smedley
Benito I. Aguirre	Sharyne L. Johnson	Thomas L. Timpe
Alicia Alcantar	**Maurice L. Landrum**	Edward A. Trujillo
Sabrina L. Barnes	Curtis W. Lawson	Craig W. Tucker
Patrick A. Barrett	Cynthia D. LeGardye	Eric C. Williams
John Berdin	Joan C. Leuck	Johanna K. Williams
Andrew J. Blanch	Gregory J. Macias	Tamara S. Williams
V. LaShay Brown	Monte L. Mahan	Denny L. Dillard
Retha D. Camp	Sean A. Mahoney	Ronald E. Marbrey
Eugene W. Coleman	James J. Marstell	Tanya R. Bobo
Michael G. Daly	Jorge L. Martinez	Dana Cash
Ruben Escoto	Howard D. Mathew	Robert V. Fox
Kemp C. Fairbanks	Belinda R. Matranga	
Kimberleigh Fletcher	Thomas J. McDonald	

Jacqueline Franklin

Lance Franscell

LaWanda Gage

Shelley A. Gale

Patricia L. Garcia

Jeffrey V. Ghan

Stephen C. Godlewski

Miles O. Hawkes

Mary F. Hodge

Thomas G. Hromada

Raymond S. Jatkowski

Carmen M. Johnson

Edwin Melendez

Alexander S. Moreno

Ann C. Munch

David G. Nunez

Whitney J. Pauly

John M. Pingel

Edgelbelt R. Quechenberger

James W. Radtke

Antonio Ramirez

Lynn E. Reum

Kenneth A. Saucier

Paul L. Skinner

ABOUT THE AUTHOR

I n 1959, I was born in Los Angeles, California, at John Wesley County Hospital. During that time, my father, Maurice L. Landrum Sr., worked for the city of Los Angeles Department of Parks and Recreation, and my mother, Katie B. Landrum, was a stay-at-home wife and parent.

According to my certificate of birth, we resided at 11201 Zamora Avenue, Los Angeles, in William Nickerson Gardens Public Housing Development, commonly referred to as Nickerson Gardens, which opened in 1955. Designed by the black architect Paul Revere Williams, it is the largest public housing development west of the Mississippi River with 1,066 units. By the time I started kindergarten, my parents had purchased our first home in Compton, California.

They met during a birthday party hosted at the home of my Aunt Clara Cox in Los Angeles. My mother had recently moved to California from Texas to continue her education. My father had recently enlisted in the United States Marine Corps after graduating from high school. They got married before his deployment to defend our nation during the Korean War Conflict. During the early 1950s, it was considered honorable for young men to enlist in the armed services and fight for our nation. After completing his service and returning to the United States, he was honorably discharged from the Marine Corps. A couple of years later, I was born.

Several historical events took place during 1959. In January 1959, Fidel Castro came into power after a Communist revolution occurred in Cuba. Also that month, President Dwight D. Eisenhower, proclaimed Alaska, as the 49th state of the United States, and Juneau became its capital. By March 1959, the United States House of Representatives and the United States Senate approved Hawaii for statehood making it the 50th state. NASA introduced our first American astronauts, including John H. Glenn Jr. and Alan B. Shepard Jr., and the printing company Xerox launched the first commercial copier.

CHAPTER 1
Childhood Dreams

My childhood dream and desire had always been to become a police officer. It all started in kindergarten when I attended Tibby Elementary School in Compton, California. I was five years old, when my kindergarten teacher, Mrs. Wong, asked the entire class, "What do you want to be when you grow up?" I remember raising my hand and telling Mrs. Wong, "I want to be a police officer when I grow up!"

So, even at the tender age of five, I knew without a shadow of a doubt that I wanted to be a police officer. In fact, I tell people today that if I had to choose again, I still would pursue my chosen profession as a Los Angeles Police Officer. It is rare that you get a chance to live out your dream!

When I was a young child, my father would take me along to visit his friend, Police Sergeant Joel, who worked for the Compton Police Department. Sergeant Joel was a mountain of a man, who often would kid around with me, asking me if I wanted to be a junior police officer. Of course, my answer was always, "Yes, Sir." On occasion, Sergeant Joel would give me a Compton Police Department Junior Police Officer's badge. It was these positive interactions at such a young age that paved the way for me and played a major role in my decision to become a Los Angeles Police Officer.

In 1963, after the birth of my younger brother, James, our parents legally separated and would eventually file for divorce. My mother maintained full custody of the three of us: James, me, and my older sister, Kathy. So, as a single parent, she worked hard and moved our family to the planned housing community Park Village, located in Compton, California.

Our home address was 515 Corregidor Street. I attended Park Village Elementary School, where I met my childhood friends, Mark and Roy. Years later, Roy would be shot and killed, and Mark ended up in state prison for murder. We were "the three amigos" as childhood friends. We attended the same elementary school and played little league baseball together.

NOTE TO PARENTS: One of the best ways to keep your children out of street gangs and trouble is to engage them in organized recreational sports! My mother adopted that philosophy as a single parent and made sure that my brother and I stayed busy playing youth sports.

Dead Body

One afternoon while walking to the baseball park located on Alondra Boulevard, south of Compton High School, Roy and I noticed a large puddle of bright red blood on the sidewalk. Being curious youngsters, we decided to follow the blood trail. It led us into an apartment complex courtyard off of the main thoroughfare. There we saw a black male adult lying on the ground in a puddle of blood; he was staring into space with his eyes wide open. His body looked as stiff as a board. A small crowd had gathered, and someone whispered that the man had been shot while attempting to break into a nearby apartment. This was the first time I would see a dead body. Unfortunately, it would not be my last!

Shortly after that incident, my mother sat me down and told me about the senseless shooting death of our neighborhood Helm's Bakery deliveryman. The crime occurred early one morning while we were in school during the commission of an armed robbery in Park Village. Hearing about this death left me feeling sad. He was a nice man just trying to make an honest living. Shortly after that incident, my mother decided it was time for us to move out of Compton to the Greater San Fernando Valley.

The Greater San Fernando Valley

During the early summer of 1970 like the Beverly Hillbillies, we packed up our family and moved to the Pierce Street Park Apartments, located in Pacoima, California, which was consisted one of the oldest neighborhoods in the northern San Fernando Valley.

Living in Pacoima was different than living in Compton. Pacoima was a much larger city and covered 7.1 square miles with a population of 81,000, which equated to about 10,000 people per square mile. Compton was much smaller in terms of the population. The onsite manager for the Pierce Street Park Apartments drove around in his golf cart armed with a .45-caliber pistol. Our apartment complex was directly across the street from Charles Maclay Junior High School. I remember my brother and I participated in the summer recreational program, which consisted of swimming, playing board games, basketball, softball, and dodge ball. We enjoyed a great first summer, and my mother enrolled us into a private Christian school, the San Fernando Valley Academy (SFVA). We remained enrolled in SFVA until my mother could no longer afford to pay our tuition.

San Fernando Earthquake, aka Sylmar Earthquake

On February 9, 1971, at approximately 6:01 a.m., the greater San Fernando Valley experienced a major earthquake. Due to its epicenter and vast destruction, it was dubbed The Sylmar Quake. The devastation was overwhelming, especially at the San Fernando Veterans Administration Hospital, which was built in 1926. Several of the building's concrete wings collapsed, trapping and killing 44 people.

This was my first experience living through a major earthquake, which killed people, damaged and destroyed homes, apartments, freeways, and roadways. The Olive View Hospital that was built to withstand a major earthquake was destroyed. Shortly after the earthquake, my mother purchased a home on Judd Street in Pacoima, California. In the meantime, my father had remarried and was living in the city of Sylmar on Corcoran Street, approximately one mile away.

Even though we lived about a mile from my father, we hardly saw him. That was very disheartening to me as a young child. At the time I played minor league baseball and was pretty good at it.

I managed to make the baseball all-star teams wherever I played. The only thing missing was my father's physical presence. During that period, my father worked for the Department of Water and Power as a Lineman.

I do recall during one of my baseball games, my father drove up in a large Department of Water and Power truck, parked along the outfield, and watched the game. I was excited my father had finally made one of my games. I recall stepping into the batter's box, waiting on the pitch and hitting a homerun. Talk about being fired up! I looked up only to notice my father had already driven away. I shared the majority of my baseball accolades with my teammates. Unfortunately (and fortunately), my mother was busy working as the primary care provider to keep a roof over our heads, food on the table, and clothes on our back.

When my mother reached the point where she could no longer afford to live in California, she decided to relocate us to Austin, Texas, where her family, the Davidsons, lived. Before moving to Texas, my oldest sister and her boyfriend got married. My mother allowed us to finish the school year in good old Southern California. As soon as school was over, we were on our way to Austin, Texas. Upon our arrival, we stayed with one of my mother's older sisters (there were eleven siblings), Aunt Tea Baby. That's right. You read it correctly. Back in those days, families had nicknames for everyone. Aunt Tea Baby had a heart the size of Texas. Although she is no longer here on this earth, I love her and will always be forever grateful for everything my Aunt Tea Baby did for our family.

Texas and a Painful Lesson

Once we moved to Austin, my mother applied for employment at Brackenridge Hospital, where she was hired as a nurse's aide. We eventually moved into an apartment in a subdivision of Austin called Metropolis. I went to Porter Junior High School and played tackle football. Upon graduating from Porter, I attended Del Valle High School, where I continued to play football.

One of my most unforgettable memories involves receiving two swats after making a poor command decision to leave early for lunch following fourth period gym. Normally, everyone lined up and sprinted to the cafeteria for lunch. The lines were always long, so if you left early, you could avoid the long wait. On this particular day, I decided to line up and leave for lunch about three minutes early. Well, for some reason, Coach Taylor decided to take roll again at the end of class. Needless to say, he marked me absent for the day, which meant you either had to get a written note from your parent(s) or receive a couple of swats to avoid that. I selected option two.

So, picture in your mind, Coach Taylor, a big man, approximately 6'4", 250 pounds with 18-inch-thick arms. The wooden paddle used in those days had dozens of dime size holes that would absorb your butt cheeks for maximum pain and effect. There was nothing good about option two, but I did not want to get my mother involved or cause her to miss work, because of my poor decision to leave for lunch three minutes early.

School Discipline

That fateful day, I recall that I was wearing a pair of thin double-knit brown trousers even though the temperature was in the mid-forties. I walked into Coach Taylor's office, and he explained how he would erase the absence mark in his roll call attendance book if I agreed to take two swats. Otherwise, I would have to get a note from my mother to justify my absence. Since, I never caused my mother any problems, I decided to accept the swats as my punishment. However, in the back of my mind, I was thinking: bad idea. Coach Taylor's office faced the gymnasium and through the blinds looking out of his office, you could see the basketball courts.

Coach Taylor directed me to bend over and grab onto the wooden handles on his office chair. Although, I dreaded what was about to happened, I wanted to get it over with. So, Coach Taylor, positioning himself as if he were sighting in a brand new firearm, placed the paddle on my butt for a reference point. The next thing I knew, BOOM! The first strike, I immediately grabbed my butt to hold myself up. I only weighed about 95 pounds soaking wet back then. I had tears in my eyes, but did not want to show weakness. My butt felt like a burning furnace. Coach Taylor looked at me and had the nerve to say, "Son, this could have been two quick swats!" Apparently, he hadn't noticed my butt was on fire after his first ballistic strike. I reluctantly grabbed hold of the chair and held on for dear life for the final strike. BOOM! Coach Taylor lit me up again. I thought my pants were on fire.

I forgot all about lunch. Instead, I spent the entire lunch period walking around the basketball court in the gymnasium holding my backside. I was desperately attempting to regain the feeling in my butt as well as practicing how to sit in a chair for my fifth period class without being in pain. I learned a painful lesson that day and never left early for lunch again. In fact, it never crossed my mind, but the memory of Coach Taylor lighting up my butt has remained as vivid a memory as if it were yesterday.

First Summer Job

After the school year was over, I was hired through the Summer Youth Employment Program for my first summer job as a student worker at Stephen F. Austin High School. I remember making my lunch, which consisted of a couple of peanut butter sandwiches, some chips and a piece of fresh fruit. I rode the bus daily and exited near the state's capital, which was a couple of blocks from the high school. That summer, I worked for the field maintenance supervisor. In fact, I was the only employee. I remember him handing me a wrench and directing me to tighten all the bolts in the football stadium's bleachers. I was like, "What the hey-hey!" The stadium was freaking huge. Did I mention that the stadium was freaking huge and the temperature was Gatorade hot?

I was pretty motivated at the beginning. However, Mr. Sun began to beam down on me and have an impact on my desire to do that type of labor. As the morning went on, it became evident that I was not cut out for this line of work.

That sort of manual labor at the age of 14 was too much for this California native. So, when it was time for lunch, I politely walked into the work shed, grabbed my lunch, walked out, and ate it while on the way home. That's right, I quit my first summer job on the first day. No two-week notice, not even a two-minute notice, I was out of there quicker than you could say, "What's for lunch, homeboy?"

We continued to live in Texas, until I finished ninth grade, then my mother decided it was time for us to move back to California. I think she missed my oldest sister, Kathy, who had given birth to my first nephew, Dante. The move was welcome news for my younger siblings and I. Texas during that time was a hot mess!

CHAPTER 2
Back to California

In the summer of 1975, we started our road trip back to California. My mother allowed me drive on and off during the journey. When we arrived in California, we landed at my sister's apartment, located at 4114 Buckingham Road, Los Angeles, California. Today, that neighborhood is known to as, "Baldwin Hills Village." However, back then, it was affectionately referred to as, "The Jungle" because of the numerous apartment complexes, pools, palm trees, and foliage. The Jungle was developed in the 1950s when the crime rate was low to accommodate single adults and families.

We stayed with my sister, her husband, and my oldest nephew through the summer before my mother decided Long Beach was the next stop on our life's journey. She was able to secure Section 8 housing, financial assistance, and food stamps, and for approximately two-weeks, we lived at a housing shelter in Long Beach on Daisy Avenue near 8th Street.

That experience was really humbling. I knew my mother was doing the best she could for us as a single parent. The welfare assistance allowed her to put a roof over our heads and food on the table. We ended up moving into a three-bedroom apartment at 2285 Lewis Avenue in Long Beach. The on-site manager Mrs. Maxwell was such a nice lady. She welcomed us with open arms. In addition to a daughter, she had four sons, whom my brother and I befriended. Her oldest son, James, and I were the same age.

Since we were back in California, I was anxious to reconnect with my childhood friends, Mark and Roy. One afternoon, my mother drove me over to Roy's home in Park Village. I knocked on the door, and his mother answered. I asked to speak to Roy, and his mother replied, "Roy's dead, baby. Someone shot him in the head about three years ago!" Hearing about Roy's death left me somewhat in shock. When I asked her about Mark, she replied, "Mark is in jail for murder." I was totally blown away by this news.

I realized just how blessed I was that my mother had made the decision to move us out of California just before the street gang violence epidemic evolved. Looking back now, all I can say is God had a different plan for me. I could have just as easily gotten caught up in that life.

As I mentioned earlier, my mother made it a point to keep my brother and I engaged in sports, like baseball, football, and karate. I remember signing up to compete in the annual Ed Parker's International Karate Tournaments held at the Long Beach Arena. Bruce Lee was my favorite martial artist. I still remember going to the Imperial Movie Theater in downtown Long Beach to watch *Enter The Dragon* and *Return of The Dragon* starring Bruce Lee.

I especially loved his character in the "Green Hornet" television series. My grand master karate instructor was Tom White. The techniques we learned were for keeps. In fact, during one of our karate sessions, my immediate karate instructor, Raymond Wilson, gave his own nephew a black eye.

I had already taken Chinese Kenpo while living in Los Angeles at the Crenshaw YMCA. So, adding the hard fighting style of Shin Ryu Karate provided me with many defensive options, not to mention discipline and patience. At one point, when I fought on the circuit, I was ranked fourth in the Martial Arts Rating System (MARS) within the state of California.

High School Years & Racial Unrest

Although, I lived approximately 1.5 miles from Long Beach Polytechnic High School (LB Poly), my neighborhood was a part of the district's remapping plan. Instead of attending LB Poly, I attended Lakewood High School, miles away. So, every morning, I caught the school bus at the corner of Hill Street and Orange Avenue and traveled to Lakewood High School, located at 4400 Briercrest Street in Lakewood. My siblings and I were among the first class of majority (Black) students to be bused into Lakewood High School. Of course, racism would rear its ugly head. There were a series of small, racially related incidents that escalated tensions over several years. I recall arriving at school one early morning via the bus and observing that someone had vandalized the school overnight with a bunch of racial slurs, swastikas, and the letters *"KKK"* spray painted on the walls of the school's main entrance. As we began to exit the bus, a scrimmage line of Los Angeles County Sheriff's Deputies had been deployed to keep the peace.

"These people are stupid. I'm embarrassed, and they should be too! I'm here to support you guys."

As we entered the school's quad area, I remembered a male White student, Joseph "Joe" Luyben, walked over and stood next to me. Joe and I were friends. He looked at me and stated, "These people are stupid. I'm embarrassed, and they should be too! I'm here to support you guys." Imagine being bused into a predominantly White neighborhood and experiencing racial prejudice coupled with civil unrest. Joe stood up that day and earned my respect. Years later, our paths would cross again, and I would return the favor to him while working at Dodger's Stadium.

During the racial unrest incident that day, several arrests were made. In fact, one of the male students on our bus apparently brandished a small-caliber handgun. The Los Angeles County Sheriff's Department arrested dummy as soon as he exited the bus. In addition to being arrested, he was expelled from Lakewood High School. In police work, we referred to such irresponsible actions as "Straight Up Felony Stupid."

Several months after the racial unrest, I was involved in a separate incident with the school's so-called bully, who had called me a derogatory racial slur using the n-word during our afterschool gymnastics practice. He challenged me to a fight and wanted to meet me the following afternoon after school. Well, first and foremost, I was the wrong person to challenge back then. I went home and told my mother what had transpired, and she recommended that I report the incident to the school's administration. My mother gave me good, sound advice, which I did not follow. I was determined to meet him to handle my business. So, immediately after school that day, I began to walk over to our agreed-upon meeting spot.

When I peeked around the corner, I observed a large, angry mob of teenagers and some adults. It was apparent no one in that group had my health and safety in mind. Obviously, Mrs. Landrum didn't raise a fool, so, I caught a ride home with some former classmates, Lawrence Arwine and his older brother. The following day, I walked to my fifth-period class and observed the challenger, who said to me, "Where were you yesterday, [n-word]?" I replied, "How about meeting me today immediately following fifth period?" Of course, he replied, "I have something to do after class today, [n-word]!" The third time he referred to me, as an n-word was the charm. Without considering the consequences, I struck him in the nose with a clenched fist. The force of my punch served its purpose; I broke his nose and promptly walked myself into the principal's office and sat there. Moments later, the bully was escorted into the nurse's office holding his bloody nose.

I apologized to Mr. Nelson Judd, the principal, for my actions and explained what the challenger had said to me and what had transpired the previous day. Mr. Judd advised me that I should have notified my teacher or someone else in authority. Mr. Judd's advice sounded familiar; it was exactly what my mother had recommended that I do the day before. In any event, I received a two-day's suspension for my poor judgment.

The challenger, on the other hand, was expelled from Lakewood High School. After that incident, I never had any more racial issues or incidents at Lakewood High School. I continued my high school experience and went on to participate in several high school sports.

Moore League Champions

As a sophomore, I made the track team at Lakewood High School. In 1976, we had a pretty good group of athletes and were crowned Moore League Champions for outperforming all the local high school competition in our league, which included Long Beach Polytechnic High School, Milliken High School, Jordan High School and Compton High School. By January 1977, I had earned enough high school credits to graduate early. So, I decided to enroll in adult night school at Woodrow Wilson High School in Long Beach and work full-time to help my mother.

South Bay Regional Academy

After graduating from high school, I enrolled in Long Beach Business Technical College and learned keypunch. I went on to work several jobs as a keypunch operator and eventually enrolled in the South Bay Regional Academy at El Camino College, in Torrance, California. This was my first official step toward becoming a Los Angeles Police Officer.

The course on law enforcement procedures and laws at South Bay was 12 credits and was taught by two Los Angeles police lieutenants, Ed Watkins and Bob Barker, and a Los Angeles County Deputy District Attorney (DDA) Dave Coffey. It was DDA Coffey who inspired me to apply for the Los Angeles Police Department. Originally, I was going to apply as a Reserve Police Officer for Culver City Police Department. DDA Coffey asked me a simple question: "Do you want to make law enforcement a career?" I replied, "Sir, that is all I want to do for a living." DDA Coffey suggested I apply for the Los Angeles Police Department instead of applying to the Culver City Police Department. I had thrived in the course academically and was elected as the class president. In retrospect, DDA Coffey gave me sound advice.

CHAPTER 3

Beginning The Process

S o, nineteen years after announcing I wanted to be a police officer, my journey was underway to become a Los Angeles Police Officer. The process
started with filling out an application at the city of Los Angeles Personnel Department, taking a written test followed by an entry-level oral interview,
performing a physical fitness agility test, undergoing a medical examination and
psychological test, and completing a thorough pre-employment background
investigation. This process took about eight months to complete. In 1983,
Daryl F. Gates was the Chief of Police for the Los Angeles Police Department
and Tom Bradley was the Mayor of Los Angeles. The two men had an inimical
working relationship, which, unfortunately, played out publicly.

Selecting the Los Angeles Police Department

I asked myself this question: Out of all of the law enforcement agencies in the
world, why become a Los Angeles Police Officer? My answer was simple. For
starters, becoming a Los Angeles Police Officer was etched in tradition; it's a
career geared specifically for professional men and women. The Los Angeles
Police Department, founded in 1869, encompassed over 468 square miles and
provided a tradition of service unlike any other large city law enforcement
agency. The LAPD's mission statement and core values were created to help
safeguard the lives and property of the citizens of Los Angeles.

In essence, "Protect and Serve" was more than just a slogan; it was considered the Los Angeles Police Department's philosophy. Service to the community truly meant protecting everyone who lived, worked, and visited the city of Los Angeles.

LAPD's Mission Statement

It has always been the mission of the LAPD to safeguard the lives and property of the people it serves, to reduce the incidence and fear of crime, and to enhance public safety while working with diverse communities to improve their quality of life. Our mandate was to do so with honor and integrity, while at all times conducting ourselves with the highest ethical standards to maintain public confidence.

Core Values

The Los Angeles Police Department's Core Values were introduced to guide and inspire its police officers in all they say and do. The Core Values have been woven into our day-to-day mission and is our mandate to help ensure that we demonstrate professional behavior. Those Core Values include:

- ► Service to Our Communities
- ► Reverence for the Law
- ► Commitment to Leadership
- ► Integrity in All We Say and Do
- ► Respect for People
- ► Quality through Continuous Improvement

Looking Back at 1983

Let's talk about a couple of things that occurred in 1983. Vanessa Williams became the first African American Miss America. Crack cocaine was developed in the Bahamas and illegally smuggled and was being distributed throughout the United States.

Our nation elected a movie star by the name of Ronald Reagan as president of the United States; Courken George Deukmejian Jr. served as governor of California. On April 4, 1983, NASA launched the first Space Shuttle, Challenger. Equally important, in November 1983, President Ronald Reagan signed legislation making the third Monday in January, a legal holiday to commemorate Dr. Martin Luther King Jr. Tom Bradley was the mayor of Los Angeles, and Venice Beach was the second largest tourist attraction within Southern California, just behind "the happiest place on Earth," Disneyland.

During this time, I lived in Long Beach, California. One week before I began the academy, my then wife and I decided to separate. My daily motivation to graduate came from my nine-month-old daughter. She was my only child at that point, and it was my job to take care of her.

The biggest influence in my life was my father, Maurice L. Landrum Sr. (RIP, Semper Fi). My dad was there for me from day one. Often, he would drive me to the Academy on his way to work. In fact, he had temporarily separated from his wife and stayed with me until I graduated from the Academy. I remember the look on his face when my name was called during my graduation ceremony. He purchased my first back-up weapon; a Smith and Wesson two-inch barrel .38-caliber revolver, as well as, my Level II T-shirt Ballistic Vest. I still own the revolver to this day!

LAPD vs. City Hall

In 1983, there were some interesting dynamics occurring within the city of Los Angeles and the LAPD. As with any big city, Los Angeles had its share of politics and drama. I remember Chief Daryl F. Gates and Mayor Tom Bradley having a war of words that played out in the local media. During that time, every potential LAPD recruit academy class had to be approved by Mayor Bradley. I was put on standby for Class 03-83. Two months later, I was hired and entered the academy as part of Class 05-83.

At that time, I learned about the civil lawsuit Hunter/La Ley v. City of Los Angeles. In short, several civil rights groups sued the Los Angeles Police Department for discriminating against African American, Latino, Asian American police officers and women. The lawsuit resulted in a federal consent decree that directed the city of Los Angeles and the Los Angeles Police Department to enforce equal pay, promotional opportunities and the hiring of African Americans, Latinos and Asian Americans, including female police officers.

Chief Gates navigated through several glitches throughout his tenure as chief of police. First, Proposition 13 impacted the department's budget and cut the sworn officer ranks to approximately 6,900; in comparison the New York Police Department, which had approximately 28,700 sworn police officers. Even the Chicago Police Department had more police officers than LAPD during the 1980s. There was a saying that resonated throughout the Los Angeles Police Department:

"When it came to handling calls for service and crime suppression, Los Angeles Police Officers have always been called upon and expected to do more with less resources."

In other words, violent street crimes did not decrease during that time period. In fact, calls for service and gang-related homicides increased. However, LAPD officers were expected to work harder with fewer officers and resources at their disposal. So, needless to say, Chief Gates had a lot on his plate, including the federal consent decree to hire and promote more African Americans, Latinos, Asian Americans and female police officers.

Another interesting dynamic during this turbulent time was the economy; the real estate market had tanked. In fact, I recalled one of my classmates driving up to the academy on day one in his four-door, burgundy Mercedes Benz. I asked why he had chosen this line of work. He was very candid with me and replied that he applied to be a Los Angeles Police Officer after the real estate market had crashed. He had been a real estate broker and needed a job with benefits to support his family. I clearly understood his point of view!

I thought to myself, what an interesting reply. I applied for this position because it was my desire to become a police officer to help the weak and arrest predators who prey upon them. Somehow, my classmate did not share that same passion or mindset. I felt humbled about being given the privilege to serve the community and wear the badge as a proud member of the Los Angeles Police Department. Unfortunately, the real estate broker would eventually be washed out of the academy, which came as no surprise to me. During my tenure, the LAPD was looking for Pride, Integrity, and Guts (PIGS).

Just imagine working for one of the largest police department's in the world. In 1983, there were approximately 7,200 sworn officers. In 2020, there are approximately 10,000 sworn officers within the rank and file of the Los Angeles Police Department.

When it came to training, I can tell you firsthand, without a doubt, the Los Angeles Police Department prepares their recruit officers to handle any day-to-day street situations (commonly referred to as "police work.") The Academy's training curriculum was broken down into three key learning domains: Criminal Law, Self Defense, and Weaponry.

By the time we graduated from the Los Angeles Police Academy, we were able to engage multiple deadly threats based on our firearms training and perform under stressful conditions.

Recruit Class 4-68 proudly dedicated the above sign that hangs over the exit door of the main hallway next to the Physical Training Staff's Office in the gymnasium. That was just one of the many signs posted throughout the academy to remind you of the blood, sweat, and tears shed by others who came before you, endured, and earned the right to be called Los Angeles Police Officers.

CHAPTER 4

The Los Angeles Police Academy

ATTENTION IN THE COMPOUND: "My name is Officer Bob Farley, and I will be the primary drill instructor during the next six months for Class 05/83. Some of you standing here before me will not graduate as Los Angeles Police Officers. You will be washed out. This job isn't for everyone!"

Welcome to the Los Angeles Police Academy, 1880 Academy Road. It's May 2, 1983, 0700 hours. I'm standing in the gymnasium along with my other classmates, having a casual conversation. Suddenly, in walk class instructors, Los Angeles Police Officer III Bob Farley and Police Officer III John Chamberlain. Their uniforms are immaculate (no Irish pendants), their nametags, badges, and shoes are perfectly shined. If there was ever a prototype of what Los Angeles police officers should look like, Farley and Chamberlain were definitely it. They called us to order and told everyone to stand at attention on the black line in a U-configuration.

Farley and Chamberlain began walking up and down the line stopping in front of each and every one of us. I was never in the military, but it surely felt like I was. I vividly recall standing near one of my classmates when Farley stopped in front of him and stared at the corduroy blazer he had worn.

Farley: "Son, where are you from?

My classmate: "I'm from Wisconsin, sir!"

Farley: "Son, why are you wearing a smoking jacket and cowboy boots?"

My classmate: "It's all I had to wear, sir!"

Farley: "Well don't wear that outfit again, not even to court!"

My classmate: "Yes sir!"

By that time, Chamberlain had ordered several of my classmates who had been laughing into the push-up position. Now keep in mind, this was only day one. We were all in for a long and interesting six months. This was boot camp LAPD-style.

What made it interesting, we all signed up to earn the right to be called, Los Angeles Police Officers! Officer Farley formally introduced himself and stated, "I will be your primary drill instructor during the next six months for Class 05/83. Some of you standing here before me will not graduate as Los Angeles Police Officers. You will be washed out. This job isn't for everyone!" Meanwhile, I remember looking to my left and right, thinking to myself, Farley must be talking to someone else, because my plan, dream, desire and goal was to graduate from the Los Angeles Police Academy as a Los Angeles Police Officer. It was my childhood dream, and nothing or nobody was about to stand in my way.

Suddenly, Police Officer III John Chamberlain, the second class instructor, joined Officer Farley as they formally inspected my classmates and I while we stood at attention on the "black line" in the gymnasium. We were referred to as Recruit Officers. Class 05-83 started out with 72 recruit officers; however, after day one, that number dropped to 69 recruit officers. Several of my classmates figured out they were not cut out for the academy. This was not just another job, it was a career and one that could get you killed if you made the wrong decision or became the unfortunate victim of an ambush. Reality began to settle in. This was the real deal. If your mindset and soul weren't right, it was time for you to excuse yourself from this reality, pain, and disappointment.

This was going to be a marathon, and my classmates and I were in it for the long haul! The official term for unsatisfactory recruit officers who left was "washed up." The philosophy behind the LAPD "stress academy" was to ensure that you would be ready and able to handle yourself under any stressful situation while remaining calm in the face of chaos. Being able to respond effectively during a life-threatening incident was paramount. Over the next 24 weeks, the academy would shape and mold us like clay into hardcore Los Angeles Police Recruit Officers.

Our self-defense instructors drilled into our heads that under no circumstances were we to tie up with a suspect. We were taught how to effectively use our department-issued PR-24 aluminum batons to gain compliance and control of an uncooperative or combative suspect. Unfortunately, use-of-force incidents occurred with regularity while handling calls for service and arrests.

Week Two

Week two was the beginning of our physical training (PT). One of the things, I did prepare for was the physical aspect of the police academy. Prior to being hired, I was running three miles a day and doing two hundred push-ups and sit-ups daily. Let's just say my decision and dedication to do that was a good thing.

Let me introduce you to PT instructor, Police Officer III Mike Diaz. He was an animal. Officer Diaz, a decorated Los Angeles Police Officer, ran the fudge out of us. In fact, we ran until buttermilk was running out of our coolers. There are several famous running trails surrounding the Los Angeles Police Academy that were used for training: Cardiac Hill, Stairway to Heaven, The Double Baxtons, and the Billy Goat Trail. By week 23, if you were fortunate enough to have survived, you would be allowed to participate in the Class' Pride Run, which started at the Academy to the fountain at Riverside Avenue and Los Feliz Boulevard and back.

As I mentioned earlier, recruit training was broken down into three separate phases: Criminal Law, Self Defense, and Weaponry. We would spend the next 960 hours honing in on all three of those learning domains. Our primary self-defense instructor, Officer Diaz, taught us about street survival, how to properly use our batons, handcuffs, wristlocks, twist locks, and, of course, the controversial choke hold. We shot our department-approved Smith & Wesson .38-Caliber Revolvers almost daily.

Our firearm instructors taught us the five-point safety check for the department's Ithaca 12-gauge shotgun. Remember the television show, *Dragnet?* Well, Joe Friday, whose actual name was Jack Webb, funded the video training room also named after him. We all spent numerous hours in that room learning the California Vehicle Code, as well as, taking exams related to the criminal laws, policies, rules, and procedures of the Los Angeles Police Department.

Physical Training aka "PT"

Suspects weren't apologetic about disarming you or trying to kill you! So, we trained every-day as though our lives depended on it. During my career on numerous occasions, my life did depend on it!

As a recruit officer, you were in the best physical shape of your life. There was definitely something to be said about doing physical fitness as a recruit officer. The running, pushups, sit-ups and self-defense tactics sharpened our minds and bodies. With each passing day, you felt the confidence growing within you. Most of us looked forward to the physical training. The military cadences during the runs—or what we referred to as, "organized foot pursuits"—had gotten easier for most of us. We would yell out at the top of our lungs, "PT, good for you, good for me, one mile, no sweat, two miles, no sweat, three miles, no sweat, PT, we love it!" We were expected to excel during all facets of physical training. Especially during our organized foot pursuits, so, we sucked it up. No excuses!

My Personal Philosophy: "If I had to chase you for a block, half mile, or whatever the distance, when it came time for you to be taken into custody, if you resisted, you could expect a good old-fashioned, LAPD style ass whipping combined with a pair of Peerless handcuffs, as well as, a few lumps and soreness to go along with your booking number!"

My mindset from day one was suspects would always pick the time and place to fight you. So, we had to stay patrol ready! My personal philosophy: If I had to chase you for a block, half mile, or whatever the distance, when it came time for you to be taken into custody, if you resisted, you could expect a good old-fashioned, LAPD-style ass whipping combined with a pair of Peerless handcuffs, as well as a few lumps and soreness to go along with your booking number!"

Working the streets of Los Angeles in the early eighties and nineties was all about street survival, especially when it came to violent confrontations with suspects. We were reminded daily during our self-defense, physical training, and firearm training that suspects weren't apologetic about disarming you or when attempting to kill you! So, we trained everyday as though our lives depended on it. On numerous occasions during my tenure with the LAPD, my life *did* depend on it! Real talk!

We were trained to deal with problems quick, fast, and in a hurry. While in the Academy, if you were performing self-defense techniques half-ass, you were probably going to get it handed to you in the streets. I took self-defense training seriously along with our firearms marksmanship training. The entire Academy experience was something that I was definitely built for, especially when it came to the self-defense portion of training.

CHAPTER 5

In The Line Of Duty

I f you ever visit any Los Angeles Police Station, please pay close attention to the photographs displayed in the lobby of our fallen heroes. Always sobering for me was the list of my fellow brother and sister officers from the Los Angeles Police Department who had been killed in the line of duty before and during my 21.5 years with the LAPD. They made the ultimate sacrifice in the line of duty while protecting strangers who could not protect themselves. To this day, I still get emotional about this because I am LAPD through and through. The thin blue line runs deep, long, and strong! God bless their families, friends, and God bless the LAPD. During my tenure, we suffered the loss of two female officers to gunfire. I highlighted these two Angel's names to honor them, as well as, the other police officers tragically killed in the line of duty. Please take a moment to honor 39 fallen heroes listed. They will never be forgotten, nor will their commitment of service to the community!

Name	Rank	Date of Death	Cause
Paul L. Verna	Police Officer	06/02/1983	Gunfire
Jack V. Evans	Police Officer	10/22/1983	Motorcycle Accident
Arthur Ken Soo Hoo	Police Officer	10/29/1983	Vehicular Assault
William N. Wong	Police Officer	10/29/1983	Vehicular Assault
Duane Curtis Johnson	Police Officer	12/19/1984	Gunfire
Thomas C. Williams	Detective	10/31/1985	Gunfire
Arleigh Eugene McCree	Detective	02/08/1986	Explosive / Pipe Bomb
Ronald Lawrence Ball	Police Officer	02/08/1986	Explosive / Pipe Bomb
Randall L. Marshall	Police Officer	06/02/1987	Motorcycle Accident
James H. Pagliotti	Police Officer III	06/02/1987	Gunfire
James C. Beyea	Police Officer I	06/07/1988	Gunfire
Daniel Allen Pratt	Police Officer	09/03/1988	Gunfire
Derrick Conner	Police Officer	12/12/1988	Car Accident
Manuel Gutierrez	Police Officer	12/12/1988	Car Accident
David Lee Hofmeyer	Police Officer	12/12/1988	Car Accident
Norman D. Eckles	Detective	04/19/1989	Gunfire
Kelly Key III	Detective	12/27/1989	Gunfire
Russell Lee Kuster	Detective	10/09/1990	Gunfire
* Tina Frances Kerbrat	**Police Officer**	**02/11/1991**	**Gunfire**
Charles R. Champe	Police Officer	06/13/1991	Helicopter Accident
Gary Alan Howe	Police Officer	06/13/1991	Helicopter Accident
Edward Stefan Kislo	Police Officer	06/13/1991	Gunfire
Raymond A Messerly Jr.	Police Officer	10/22/1991	Motorcycle Accident
David Charles Seland	Police Officer	12/16/1992	Motorcycle Accident
Joe Rios	Police Officer	01/20/1993	Bike Accident
Clarence Wayne Dean	Police Officer	01/17/1994	Motorcycle Accident
*Christy Lynn Hamilton	**Police Officer**	**02/22/1994**	**Gunfire**
Charles D. Hein	Police Officer	10/22/1994	Gunfire
Gabriel Delgado Perez-Negron	Police Officer	11/04/1995	Vehicular Assault
Mario Navidad Jr.	Police Officer	12/22/1996	Gunfire
Van Derrick Johnson	Police Officer	02/05/1997	Motorcycle Accident
Steven Gerald Gajda	Police Officer	01/01/1998	Gunfire
Filberto Henry Cuesta Jr.	Police Officer	08/09/1998	Gunfire
Brian Ernest Fenimore Brown	Police Officer	11/29/1998	Gunfire
Louis Villalobos Jr.	Police Officer III+I	03/17/2000	Training Accident
Robert Joe Mata	Police Officer	09/19/2000	Car Accident
George A. Rose Jr.	Police Officer	12/09/2001	Gunfire Accidental
Abiel Barron	Detective I	06/25/2003	Traffic Accident
Ricardo Lizarraga	Police Officer	02/20/2004	Gunfire

Personal Tribute to a Fallen Hero

On June 2, 1983, exactly one month after entering the academy, we lost a valuable member of our LAPD family, Police Officer II+II Paul Verna. He was shot and killed in the line of duty during a traffic stop in the Lake View Terrace neighborhood of Foothill Patrol Division. The cowards responsible were identified as Raynard Cummings and Kenneth Gay. They were arrested, criminally charged, convicted, and sentenced. Officer Verna's senseless death resonated with my classmates and I. Several of us dedicated our Class Pride Run to him. Officer Paul Verna, we thank you from the bottom of our hearts for your dedicated service and sacrifice, sir. You will forever live in our hearts and minds!

Special thanks to LAPD Police Officer II + II Bryce Verna, son of this fallen hero for allowing me to honor his dad!

Fallen Hero

POLICE OFFICER II+II PAUL L. VERNA

EOW 06/02/1983

Physical Fitness Qualification Records

During the Academy, we all participated in three required physical fitness qualifications, commonly referred to as PFQs. The Academy was 960 hours, which equaled six months, so every two months; we were given a Peace Officer Standards and Training (POST)-certified PFQ. The maximum amount of points you could earn was 500 points. Class 05/83 had several outstanding athletes. I broke the 13-year-old pull-up record. I performed 45 pull-ups, but was given credit for 39. Two of my other classmates had exceptional PFQs as well. Eric Williams scored (three) perfect 500s on the PFQs, and Eugene Coleman broke the timed sit-up record. Police Officer III Mike Diaz presented me with this clay badge during our graduation ceremony for breaking the pull-up record.

Week 17

Training during weeks one through sixteen was geared toward week 17. From day one of the Academy, we were all told; "You must pass the Self-Defense Test in Week 17, in order to earn your badge and graduate." We were also warned that having your weapon taken away during the Self-Defense Test was an automatic disqualification/dismissal from the Academy. Passing meant you earned your badge. Needless to say, in week 17, I earned my badge. It was a major accomplishment for my classmates and I.

My First Patrol Ride-along

(Van Nuys Community Police Station)

After earning your badge, it was time to participate in the one-night ride along with a seasoned veteran Field Training Officer. So, in week 18, I was assigned to Van Nuys Patrol Division, located in Valley Bureau, for my one-night ride-along. This was all part of the Academy experience preparing you for patrol. It was like giving you a chance to apply what you had learned in the classroom during lectures and training to real life calls for service.

My ride-along was scheduled on a Friday night. I arrived at Van Nuys Community Police Station dressed, wearing my Class-A uniform, which consisted of a long sleeve wool shirt, pants and tie. I remember sitting in the front row of the roll call room with my shiny leather gear, handcuffs, and loaded firearm. It's an LAPD tradition that all "boots" or Recruit Officers sit in the front row of any LAPD roll call room. The further back you sit indicates how much time you have on the job. In my front-row seat I watched as the PM Watch Commander (W/C) entered the room and sat at his desk, facing the entire room. The W/C began to call out unit assignments and read off officer safety information from the division's patrol rotator. The rotator was used to provide officers with information about wanted suspects, crime trends, and extra patrol requests from residents and businesses within the patrol area. I was as green as they come; I wrote down my car assignment, partner's name, and unit designation into my field officer's notebook.

I was assigned to work with a seasoned veteran Field Training Officer (FTO). Once roll call was over, I stood in line at the station's kit room to sign out our Ithaca 12-gauge shotgun, two police handheld radios ("rovers") and a taser. Back in 1983, those were the tools of the trade we used to do our job. We did not have semi-automatic pistols, AR-15 long rifles or high-tech flashlights. We carried .38 caliber Smith and Wesson Revolvers, Ithaca 12-gauge shotguns and first-generation tasers. When I reflect back to sitting in the passenger's seat of my patrol car setting up the Daily Field Activities Report (DFAR), aka Patrol Log, my immediate goals were to tactically survive my first tour of duty and properly document the 525 minutes of patrol time. The DFAR was broken down into several statistical categories, (i.e., radio calls, observations, traffic enforcement, observation, arrests, etc.).

During that period, Van Nuys Patrol Division, as it was referred to back then, was not a hot bed for violent crime. The radio wasn't as busy as it would be if assigned to South Bureau. However, the danger was all the same! I advised my partner that I had not purchased my back-up weapon yet. He acknowledged me, placed his pipe in his mouth and drove us out of the station's parking lot. I knew right then and there, it was going to be a long 525 minutes. However, I was now rolling in a marked black and white police vehicle as a member of the Los Angeles Police Department. How cool is this? I thought.

Van Nuys Patrol Division—now referred to as Van Nuys Community Police Station—was responsible for police services to the communities of Sepulveda, Sherman Oaks, Valley Glen, Van Nuys, Ventura Business District, and West Van Nuys. It covered approximately 30 square miles and provided service to approximately 325,000 residents. Each neighborhood was broken down into what was referred to as a reporting district or RDs. Each RD has a basic patrol car assigned to handle calls for service in that particular RD. Shown here are the RD and basic car maps for Van Nuys Community Police Station.

Van Nuys Area Reporting District Map

PCP Suspect

As I cleared us over the radio via Communications Division, we received the following radio call: "9A23, 9A23, handle this call first. Citizens report a 415 man possibly on PCP standing in the driveway of the GM Van Nuys Assembly Plant, located at 5949 Van Nuys Boulevard. Suspect is described as a male, White, no shirt, wearing blue demin jeans. Your call is Code 2."

My Definition of Phencyclidine a.k.a. "PCP"

Phencyclidine (PCP) is a mind-altering drug that often leads to hallucinations and other distortions in a person's perception of reality. It has been my personal experience that many suspects under the influence of PCP gain supernatural strength and have a high tolerance for pain. PCP was originally developed in the 1950s as an intravenous anesthetic, however, due to the neurotoxic side effects, it was discontinued as an anesthetic for humans. PCP has several street names: angel dust, water, Sherman stick, embalming fluid, elephant tranquilizer, and rocket fuel. In the African American and Latino communities, PCP was referred to as all of the above. The term "Sherman stick" came about because suspects would often dip a Sherman cigarette in a small bottle of liquid PCP then smoke it. PCP smelled like Ethyl and was very toxic; even inhaling it could cause a person to experience headaches and other devastating self-effects. Unfortunately, this horrible drug impacted numerous LAPD officers, who handled it before fully learning about the devastating side effects.

Radio Call Designations

There are different types of radio call destinations. For example, a Code 2 designation means an urgent call that should be answered immediately. No red light or siren is used, and all traffic laws are observed while responding. A Code 3 designation is considered an emergency call. It must be answered immediately, but in a manner which will enable the responding unit to reach the scene quickly and as safely as possible. When given a Code 3 designation, you are exempted from provisions of the California Vehicle Code contained in Division 11. Officers sound a siren as reasonably necessary and the officer's vehicle displays a lighted red lamp visible from the front.

Any of the following calls for service justify a Code 3 response:

- ▶ A serious public hazard
- ▶ The preservation of life
- ▶ A crime of violence in progress
- ▶ An immediate pursuit
- ▶ A unit at the scene requests another unit Code 3

Keep in mind that the final decision for the use of Code 3, other than in response to a directed call for service, is made by the vehicle's operator. In addition, there are other times when a Code 3 response is warranted. For example, during a mobile field tactical response at the scene of a riotous incident, notifying Communications Division is not required.

Now that you know the differences between a Code 2 and Code 3 and the dangerous side effects associated with PCP, let's return to the call for service of the 415 man possibly on PCP at the GM Van Nuys Assembly Plant. My partner and I responded along with a couple other marked black and white units. I exited the passenger side of our patrol vehicle and observed the male White adult suspect sweating profusely with no shirt. I continued to monitor the suspect and noticed he had this thousand-mile stare on his face. Obviously, it was my first contact with someone being under the influence of PCP. My partner put on a pair of gloves, and we tactically deployed on the suspect. I grabbed the suspect's left arm, which was dripping in sweat. I directed him to place his hands behind his back while attempting to assist him. He was incoherent and did not follow any of my verbal commands or directions, so this was an opportunity to apply a twist or wristlock. The suspect displayed what I would describe as supernatural strength and flexed his arms straight out away from his sides like a cross. This knucklehead only weighed approximately 130 to 150 pounds. We used our body weight and continued to verbalize with the suspect to control and place him into custody. Another unit that responded to the scene actually handled the call. I learned later it was their Basic Car area.

Displaying patrol unit integrity was and still is a big deal among patrol officers. "Handle your area" was a familiar theme among Los Angeles Police Officers.

Handling your assigned area was important. So, we cleared and advised Communications Division that we were available for radio calls. Within minutes after clearing, we received another call for service: "9A23, 9A23. See the woman regarding a burglary at her residence. Suspect is GOA, handle this call Code 2." Upon our arrival, my partner and I met with the victim, an elderly White Female Adult, who advised us that someone had broken into her house and taken several items. My partner took this opportunity to sit down and interview the victim. In the meantime, he was driving me nuts with the pipe in his mouth sitting on her couch scratching out a Burglary Preliminary Investigation Report. I'm not exaggerating; we stayed at the victim's residence for approximately two and one-half hours.

NEWS FLASH: "My FTO milked the burglary investigation call for service like a farmer milking a cow. Which in essence, meant our night on patrol was over. Deep down inside of me, I was pissed off, but what do you do as a young recruit officer, who had only been on the job since breakfast? Absolutely nothing!"

Being young on the job then, I didn't recognize at the time that my partner was a "drone." This term was used in police work to describe someone who was burned out with police work. There are several factors that cause officers to become less productive, such as being disciplined by the department, being passed over for promotion, not being physically fit, or simply just being a coward, to name a few. When I returned to the Academy that following Monday morning, I heard all sorts of great patrol war stories from my classmates. Many of them were assigned to crime scenes, some made arrests, and one of my classmates was involved in a vehicle pursuit. The best I had to share was assisting another unit to take a PCP suspect into custody and the grand finale of my glorious ride along: watching my FTO waste our entire night pretending to conduct the world's biggest burglary preliminary investigation.

Week 24

My classmates and I were now the senior class. The perks for being the senior class meant up-front parking as well as the opportunity to proudly wearing our badges and gun belts around the Academy. It was Week 24, and we had one more ride-along to complete. My classmates and I would individually be assigned as the third person in a patrol vehicle with two-seasoned veteran FTOs.

This time around, I was assigned to Harbor Patrol Division, now referred to as Harbor Community Police Station, located at 2175 John S. Gibson Boulevard, San Pedro. Back then, it was known as, "Where the sewer meets the sea!" I got lucky this time around; I was assigned to Unit 5A1 with two outstanding FTOs. What a big difference from my initial ride-along with Officer Drone at Van Nuys Patrol Division. This time, I was riding along with two hard-charging, proactive police officers.

Harbor Community Police Station provided service to the communities of Harbor City, Harbor Gateway, San Pedro, Terminal Island, and Wilmington. It covered approximately 27 square miles and served approximately 171,000 residents. Each neighborhood was broken down into what is called a reporting District or RD. The RDs have a basic patrol car assigned to handle calls for service within a particular jurisdiction.

CHAPTER 6

Harbor Community Police Station

(Where the Sewer Meets the Sea)

I t was a sunny, breezy afternoon in San Pedro, birds chirping, music and children playing. We were headed to our Basic Car Patrol beat area. I was seated in the back seat of our marked black and white police vehicle as the third-person observer. Suddenly, Communications Division broadcast: "Any available Harbor Unit, handle this call first, 415 fight at the Kan-Kan Bar, located at 104 S. Pacific Avenue. PR reports a male armed with a pool cue stick beating another male, your call is Code 3!"

Numerous Harbor Patrol units respond to the radio call, including us. One of my FTOs advised Communications Division, "5A1, show us en-route to the

415 fight at the Kan-Kan Bar." We responded Code 3, red lights and siren on. It was better than any "E" ticket ride at Disneyland! My blood was pumping; we were rolling code to a crime in progress!

Upon our arrival, Los Angeles City Fire Department Paramedics (LAFD) were already on scene rendering medical aid to a male Hispanic adult, who was lying in a fetal position on the sidewalk motionless adjacent to the Kan-Kan Bar, bleeding profusely from the back of his head. In the meantime, other officers had begun to establish a crime scene, cordoning off the area using yellow crime scene barrier tape, which read, "Los Angeles Police Department–Police Line Do Not Cross." Located within the crime scene was a broken pool cue stick on the ground next to the victim's body. My FTOs directed me and another Police Officer I, Victor Mendoza, to canvass the immediate area for any evidence of the crime and potential witnesses. Prior to walking down the north/south alley, I overheard one of the LAFD paramedics state that the individual being treated had vital signs that were consistent with someone who had been shot as opposed to someone who had been struck in the head with a pool cue stick.

Meanwhile, Mendoza and I kept walking down the north/south alley in a southerly direction toward 2nd Street east of Pacific Avenue. As we approached 2nd Street, I observed a lady wearing a pink robe with pink rollers in her hair standing on her front porch. She began screaming at the top of her lungs, so Mendoza and I ran over to investigate what prompted her to scream. Well, to our surprise, we looked down and observed lying in her front yard, a male Hispanic adult with what appeared to be some type of puncture wound in the middle of his chest. The male was not moving, so I checked his wrist for a pulse and signs of life. I was unable to detect a pulse and requested paramedics to our location. I also notified my FTOs of what was happening. Paramedics responded and officially pronounced the male Hispanic "dead right there" (DRT).

After the paramedics pronounced him dead, I looked at Mendoza, leaned down toward the decedent's head and stated, "This guy just whispered to me, 'It's killing me to lay here like this!'" Often, police officers like myself will use humor to take our minds away from the brutality and senseless killings that we observe frequently. It helps us to complete the mission and task at hand.

A small-caliber handgun was recovered from underneath his body. Detectives responded to both crime scenes and conducted their preliminary murder investigation. During their on-scene homicide investigation, it was determined that the decedent was the second party involved in the Kan-Kan Bar shooting incident. After procuring a search warrant, we entered the Kan-Kan Bar to look for evidence of the shooting. It was determined based on the evidence located inside the bar that the entire incident had taken place inside and not outside as it had been staged to appear. It was further determined that employees of the Kan-Kan Bar had tampered with the evidence, covering up the location of the real crime scene by staging the outside crime scene to make it appear as if the fight had taken place outside instead of inside of the bar. The primary reason was, obviously, greed and to protect their liquor license.

Meanwhile, the inside of the bar looked like a scene out of war-torn Iraq. There were bullet holes everywhere and a bloody mop that had been partially hidden behind the bar. A search of the women's restroom disclosed blood splattered everywhere, including on the mirrors. I was assigned to protect the crime scene for the remainder of my shift until I was relieved at end of watch.

I stood by and waited for the Los Angeles County Coroner to respond. The Coroner Investigator's job was to conduct an on-scene investigation and document their findings. In this case, the decedents' bodies were transported to the coroner's office, located at 1104 N. Mission Road, Los Angeles, where they would undergo autopsies to determine their official causes of death. Since both victims/suspects were dead, the criminal investigation would be classified as, "Cleared other." In other words, there were no outstanding suspects. The California Department of Alcoholic Beverage Control was notified to conduct their independent investigation. The Kan-Kan Bar was fined and their liquor license was temporarily suspended. Finally, I would have something of interest to talk about with my classmates on Monday morning.

Week 25

Every Los Angeles Police Recruit Officer must learn how to properly operate a marked black and white police vehicle during a Code 3 emergency. The

Emergency Vehicle Operation Course (EVOC) provided recruit officers like me the necessary training to properly and safely operate a police vehicle in an emergency situation.

It was imperative to clearly understand the department's policy, as well as, the Division 11 of the California Vehicle Code regarding emergency vehicle operations while responding to a Code 3 with lights and siren or during a vehicle pursuit.

We were given some classroom training and then paired up with our driving instructors, who drove us around the EVOC track in Harbor Patrol Division's jurisdiction. We were shown how to activate the lights and siren. We practiced advanced steering and braking techniques as well as operating the vehicle in adverse weather and road conditions. The most important aspect of EVOC training was learning the department's Pursuit Policy to mitigate and reduce civil liability in addition to staying alive.

Of course, we were given an EVOC examination to demonstrate we understood and retained the information taught during our training. At the end of the day, I had an opportunity to operate a marked black and white police vehicle at high speeds. Driving Code 3 was definitely something we would do throughout our career as a member of the LAPD.

Tear Gas Training

Tear Gas Training Day was one of the last things left for the Class 05/83 to experience. Participation was mandatory. The primary purpose for teargas training was to become familiar with the temporary debilitating effects of tear gas upon the human body. Normally, tear gas is deployed during a SWAT call out or civil unrest situations.

We were directed to wear our physical training sweatshirt and sweat pants and to bring our tear gas mask. A couple of my classmates who had previously served in the military considered this experience just another walk in the park, especially since they'd completed military basic boot camp. We were shown how to properly put on our gas masks and check for a good seal, which meant your mask was secure around your face. Next, we were led into the gashouse like sheep headed to a slaughter. The tear gas was deployed in the gashouse, and we all walked through with our gas masks on from the front to the rear exit without any problems. I recalled holding a conversation with some of my classmates and thinking to myself, "This was easy. A piece of cake." After everyone had gone through, reality set in. All of a sudden, Officer Farley yelled out, "Line up and remove those gas masks, it's time to experience the real effects of tear gas!" Our loving, caring, and thoughtful class instructors Farley and Chamberlain had us line up to walk back through the gashouse, this time without our gas masks.

There was no talking. It was replaced by lots of coughing, choking, burning eyes, and plenty of snot running out of our noses. Farley and Chamberlain were laughing their butts off. Of course, we provided the entertainment at no charge! We were directed to use the water hose to help wash away the burning sensation and other effects from the tear gas. Mission accomplished. We were tear gas baptized!

Warner Bros. Studio Lot (Training Day)

We had an opportunity to receive some enhanced officer survival tactical training from our Los Angeles Police Metropolitan Division's Special Weapons and Tactics Unit (SWAT) during a training day on the Warner Bros. back lot in Burbank, California.

LAPD SWAT History

History Lesson: After numerous sniper attacks upon citizens and police officers before and after the 1965 Watts Riots, Metropolitan Division formed the Special Weapon and Tactics Unit. According to historical information, Police Officer John Nelson had conducted some research on special weapons and tactics and how to respond to treacherous situations. He presented his concept to an inspector by the name of Darryl F. Gates. Inspector Gates reviewed the information and eventually approved Officer Nelson's concept of deploying a small group of trained and disciplined officers that would utilize special weapons and tactics to counter unusual attacks.

According to the LAPD, the first Special Weapons and Tactics Unit consisted of fifteen four-men teams. The majority of the officers were from patrol and other assignments within the department, and all had some sort of specialized training or prior military experience. They were first identified as Station Defense Teams that provided security at police stations and were deployed during civil unrest occurrences.

By 1971, the department created Metropolitan Division, and SWAT personnel were assigned on a full-time basis to respond to a variety of dangerous crime-related issues, including barricaded suspects, high-risk search and arrest warrants, civil unrest, dignitary protection, and other incidents that required specialized tactical deployment.

LAPD SWAT members train continuously in order to respond to any tactical situation within the city of Los Angeles and outside depending on the situation. Metropolitan Division is divided into several platoons; SWAT's designation was D Platoon.

In May 1974, SWAT responded to East 54th Street and was involved in one of the most notable shootouts in LAPD's history. During the shootout with the Symbionese Liberation Army (SLA), approximately 9,000 rounds of ammunition were exchanged between SWAT and the SLA. When the smoked, all cleared six members of the SLA were dead and, amazingly, no Los Angeles police officers were shot.

During our training day, we received informative and tactical training tips to enhance our skills related to felony vehicle pullovers and other high-risk traffic stops and, more importantly, our safety. Safety was paramount as working the violent streets of Los Angeles was serious business.

"Working the violent streets of Los Angeles was serious business. It's not like playing cops and robbers. Suspects played for keeps out in the streets, so if you got caught slipping, there's no tomorrow!"

CHAPTER 7

Graduation Day

The day before graduation we were given our first Division assignments for our one-year probationary period. Back in week 18, we were directed to submit our wish list of three Patrol Divisions in preferred order. I wanted to work in South Bureau, so I selected 77th Patrol Division, Harbor Patrol Division, and, as my safety net, one West Bureau Patrol Division, Wilshire Patrol. Officer Farley entered the room and called our class to order. He began to read off our names and the Patrol Divisions we would be assigned. I listened for my name to be called. "Recruit Officer Landrum, you will be assigned to Harbor Community Police Station as a Police Officer I." Although I did not get my first choice, I was happy to be assigned to South Bureau, Harbor Patrol Division. My 63 other classmates were sent to various patrol divisions.

Chief Daryl F. Gates officiating Class 05-83's Graduation

LAPD Class 05-83

(From the Beginning to Graduation)

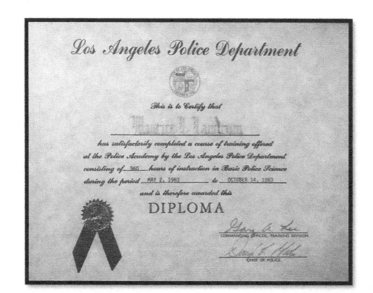

CHAPTER 8
Police Officer I

("Boot")

"Welcome to Harbor Patrol Division, where the sewer meets the sea."

H arbor Patrol Division was located at the entrance to the Port of Los Angeles, one of the busiest seaports on the West Coast. The station has been referred to as the beacon for ensuring the safety of all those who live, work, and play in the area. With a population of approximately 171,000 residents and an area of 27 squares miles, Harbor Patrol Division was the largest division within South Bureau.

Harbor Area Reporting District Map

Well, here we go folks! I successfully graduated from the Los Angeles Police Academy. My job classification changed overnight from Recruit Officer to Police Officer I. For the next twelve months, I would be a probationary officer commonly referred to as a Boot.

The term "Boot" is a military term, which meant fresh recruit out of boot camp. In my case, I was fresh out of the Los Angeles Police Academy.

Today, Harbor Patrol Division is referred to as Harbor Community Police Station. It would be my home for the next thirteen months (aka deployment periods). Within the LAPD, there was definitely a pecking order for those on probation. For example, as a Boot, you were expected to be dressed and seated upfront in the roll call room approximately 15 minutes before the start of watch.

As a PO-1, you were expected to wear and maintain your Class-A uniform: a long sleeve wool uniform shirt, wool pants, black clip-on tie and tie bar. Your leather gear, including your gun belt (a "Sam Browne" for men or "Sally Browne" for women), was expected to be squared away satisfactory or above. Your badge and nametag were expected to be clean and polished.

During roll call, Probationary Officers sat in the front two rows of the roll call room. Like I mentioned earlier, seniority was a big thing, and no one was immune from the pecking order. For instance, a Police Officer III, also referred to as a Field Training Officer (FTO), usually sat in the back row. Depending on their time on the job, there were specific seats reserved for the most senior officers, regardless of rank.

However, I did not have to worry about any of that. I was a Boot, and my place during roll call was up front. Once the Watch Commander, a Lieutenant of Police, an Assistant Watch Commander, a Sergeant II of Police entered the room, roll call was in session. The Lieutenant's unit designation for Harbor Division was 5L10.

Harbor Patrol Division operated out of Operations South Bureau (OSB). Within OSB there are four separate patrol divisions (Harbor Patrol Division, 77th Street Patrol Division, Southeast Patrol Division, Southwest Patrol Division) and one traffic division (South Traffic Division).

Shifts and Assignments

There are several different watches one could be assigned to work:

- Day watch
- Middays watch
- PM watch
- Mid-PMs watch
- Morning watch

The middays and mid-PMs were considered overlapping watches designed to provide coverage when day and PM watch officers would request lunch via the radio (Code 7). It never failed that the Sugar Honey Ice Tea always hit the fan toward end of watch. In other words, it could be quiet all shift long, and then just when it's time to go end of watch: Bang-Boom! Being assigned to morning watch at Harbor Patrol Division, I definitely had to get used to working from midnight to morning.

First Night On Probation

So, imagine working near the Pacific Ocean in October 1983. My first Field Training Officers (FTOs) were Police Officer III Jerry Doyle and Police Officer III Tom Appleby. Both Doyle and Appleby had over 25 years of service on the job. Doyle had previously been assigned to the Elite Metropolitan Division, which was home for the Los Angeles Police Department's Special Weapons and Tactics Team (SWAT), K-9 and the mounted units. Both of my FTOs were on days off for my first official night, so I worked with a veteran Police Officer II, who had several years of patrol experience.

After roll call, I stood in line at the Kit Room to check out our assigned equipment, which included our handheld radios ("ROVERS") as well as our 12-gauge Ithaca shotgun. Then, I stood in the parking lot awaiting the arrival of Unit 5A43 from PM watch.

During change of watch, you get your assigned police vehicle unless that particular unit is working overtime or the vehicle is out of service. As a rule of thumb, it was the responsibility of the unit going end of watch to ensure that the vehicle had a full tank of gasoline for the oncoming shift. It was also the end of watch unit's responsibility to clean out the interior portion of the vehicle and dispose of sunflower seeds, coffee cups or any trash generated during their tour of duty.

During our start of watch, I was responsible for inspecting our vehicle for any evidence of fresh traffic accident (T/A) collision damage and checking underneath the backseats to ensure that no evidence was hidden or left behind. Suspects will often attempt to discard their contraband in the backseat of the patrol vehicle to avoid being charged. That's why it was imperative to check the backseat after every transported or detained person was removed. After completing those tasks, it was time to prepare a Daily Field Activities Report (DFAR) to document our 525-minute shift.

I completed the vehicle inspection of our patrol vehicle and stood by for my partner. During 1984, technology wise, LAPD was approximately eight years behind. Communications Division had just installed mobile digital terminals (MDTs) in our black and white police vehicles and was in the process of programing them. So, basically, we could run vehicle license plates and check suspects' for outstanding wants and warrants. Calls for services were still being broadcast, and we were responsible for writing down the address of the call, victim name(s), witnesses, and suspect information and descriptions, as well as, the type of crime.

Shots Fired, Man with Gun

Upon signing on and clearing the parking lot, a Mid-PM watch unit requested additional units respond to their location on Santa Cruz, just east of Pacific Avenue in the alley for a 415 man shooting a firearm out of his bedroom window. Upon our arrival, the officers handling the call told my partner and I they were monitoring a suspect, who was firing his handgun from out of an upstairs' apartment bedroom window. Now, remember, this was my first official night on patrol.

As my partner was talking with the officers, when he turned to me and stated, "Call in for some help to our location." So, I followed his instructions and requested, "Help" for a 415 man shooting a firearm out of his upstairs bedroom window. I gave our location and stood by. Suddenly, all we hear are multiple sirens wailing and heading our way. My partner looked at me and asked what did you request over the radio? I responded, "Sir you asked me to call for help to our location, so I followed your instructions." He looked at me and stated, "I meant for you to request a couple of additional units." I advised Communications Division to show a Code 4 at our location, which meant we had sufficient units at the scene.

Eventually, the suspect surrendered and was taken into custody without incident after the LAPD Air Unit responded and illuminated his apartment. The firearm used by knucklehead was recovered, and he was transported and booked at the Harbor Division jail. My partner and I debriefed the situation and talked about what constitutes a call for help. For the rest of our shift, we would handle different calls for service, but nothing of significance.

Roll Call (Rotator)

During roll call we received our unit assignments. Roll call was a forum used to deploy officers to a particular beat area or patrol area. All officers were expected to have a field officer's notebook to record the date, unit designation, partner's name, and any pertinent information the Watch Commander might disseminate from the "Rotator." The Rotator contained information on wanted suspects, officer-involved shootings, extra patrol request, training and officer safety information, death and funeral notices of department personnel or family members, as well as paygrade and advancement opportunities.

My First Field Training Officer

"You've got the job unless you screw it up. It is your responsibility to keep it; officer safety and officer

survival are crucial. Report writing and handling calls for service will come with experience."

Probably one of the coolest FTOs I ever had an opportunity to work with was my first Training Officer, Jerry "Mad Dog" Doyle. On night three, I finally got to work with my assigned FTO. After roll call, I set up our patrol vehicle and waited for Doyle. After getting his serial number, I signed on via the radio to Communications Division. I told Doyle that I carried a back-up weapon and where I had it hid on my person. Doyle responded that he did not carry a back up!

Upon clearing from the station, Doyle drove us to the Tommy's Burger No. 2, located on the northwest corner of Broad Avenue and Anaheim Boulevard in Wilmington. Doyle asked me what I would like to drink. I replied, "Orange juice, sir!" He stared at me, smiled and stated, "You don't drink coffee?" I replied, "No sir!" He laughed and replied, "Oh, that will change, give this shift a couple of weeks!" It was sort of a tradition for morning watch units to meet for coffee at the start of watch if the world wasn't falling apart and to talk about a variety of subjects. Doyle took this time to talk with me about his expectations for me on probation.

He looked me in the eyes and said, "You've got the job, unless you screw it up. It is your responsibility to keep it; officer safety and officer survival is crucial. Report writing and handling calls for service will come with experience." Although I felt a slight sense of relief, I knew deep down in my soul, I hadn't proven anything yet. We cleared to handle several calls for service. As a probationary officer, you have a pecking order to abide by. For example, I wore a pair of Bally dress shoes purchased during the Academy. I wanted to purchase a pair of boots, however, I had two FTOs and wanted to make sure it was OK with them both.

I eventually got the chance to work with my other FTO, Tom Appleby. He had just rotated back into patrol after being on loan to detectives. Appleby was clean-shaven and usually wore a short-sleeve uniform shirt. In fact, it was usually freezing near the water in San Pedro during our shift. Appleby would have the windows rolled down with the air conditioner on low. At the time, I could not afford a jacket, just my Class-A uniform: a long-sleeve wool shirt with a thermal shirt underneath as well as my wool uniform pants.

God bless my mother who came to my rescue. She purchased my uniform jacket. I still remember it cost her $72 back then. I went to work that night ready for the cold. I got the car ready, sat in the passenger's seat with the windows rolled down and air conditioning system turned on low just the way Appleby liked. He got in the car, looked at me and said, "Turn the heat on and roll up your window. I'm catching a cold." In my mind I thought, "What the fudge!" I was all set for another cold night on patrol and Appleby decided he wanted the windows rolled up. That was hilarious!

Meanwhile, I had spoken to Doyle about two important personal subjects: growing my moustache and purchasing some boots to wear for patrol. About the moustache, Doyle responded, "I've never known a dude without one! It's okay with me." He also told me it would be okay to purchase a pair of department-approved boots to wear in uniform. Now keep in mind that on probation you have to play the game. Just because one FTO gives you the OK, doesn't mean the other FTO will approve. So, the next time I worked with Appleby, I told him that I had spoken to Doyle a couple of days prior about growing out my moustache and purchasing a pair of department-approved boots to wear in uniform. Appleby also gave me the thumbs up!

I immediately began to grow my moustache so that I did not look like a 10th grader any longer. I worked with Doyle and Appleby for approximately three months during phase one of my probationary period. During those three months, I would learn how to impound vehicles, complete burglary and robbery preliminary investigations, write personal citations, and properly fill out booking recommendation forms for suspects being booked into Harbor Jail. I also learned how to complete the DFAR and communicate via the radio with the assigned Police Services Representative (PSR), aka Radio Telephone Operator (RTO) at Communications Division.

Hot Prowl Burglar From Motor Vehicle Suspect

It's a cold winter night in Harbor Patrol Division; I was working with Doyle assigned to a 5A43 (San Pedro Basic Patrol Car). In any event, we received a call for service of a burglary from motor vehicle (BFMV) suspect breaking into a motorhome in the Harbor Gateway community. Doyle and I responded to the location and observed the motorhome parked on the street underneath a mercy vapor overhanging streetlight.

I requested further information from Communications Division. We were informed the suspect was inside the motorhome. Doyle and I tactically deployed on the motorhome, and we noticed that the passenger's side door was slightly ajar. Based on the circumstances, we withdrew our firearms and cautiously proceeded to enter the motorhome. Using our flashlights, we illuminated the interior. As Doyle announced our presence, we observed the suspect, who was holding a screwdriver in his right hand. Doyle ordered him to drop the screwdriver. The suspect complied, which was probably the best thing he had done in a while. He was taken into custody and escorted to our police vehicle for an all-expense paid trip to jail.

This was my first BFMV felony arrest. The suspect on this particular caper had a drug problem and felt it was easier to break into working peoples' vehicles and steal their stuff than to seek treatment. My partner told him how lucky he was to be standing in the booking cage getting booked. He had no idea how close he was to being transported to the Los Angeles County Coroner's Office.

Firearm Accidental Discharge Incident

(Internal Affairs Complaint Investigation No. 84-0521)

On December 26, 1983, I was assigned to Unit 5A43, working with Doyle. It was approximately 0500 hours, close to end of watch, when we received a radio call from Communications Division: "5A43, handle this call first. 415 man armed with a gun in the alley between 7th and 8th Streets, east of Pacific Avenue. The suspect was described as a male, Hispanic, in his late 40s. Your call is Code 2 High."

Doyle and I responded to the call within minutes. While en route, we discussed tactics. Upon our arrival, I exited our police vehicle armed with our department's Ithaca 12-gauge shotgun. I chambered a live round into the chamber and made the weapon ready for live fire. As we began to approach the location, I observed the suspect hiding behind a car in the alley. I alerted Doyle while simultaneously ordering the suspect into a felony prone position at gunpoint. He complied as Doyle, the designated contact officer, approached, handcuffed, and searched him. Doyle recovered a loaded firearm the suspect had placed underneath the vehicle he had hid behind.

Meanwhile, I was in the process of unloading the shotgun in order to reload and secure it. I had the barrel of the shotgun pointed into the sky, as we were trained, and inadvertently placed my left index finger through the trigger guard and pressed on the trigger. Boom! I was like, "Damn! What the hell just happened?" Doyle placed the suspect into the back of our police vehicle, walked over to me, took control of the shotgun, looked me in the eyes and stated, "How do you want to handle this?" Doyle gave me some good advice that day. He stated, "If it were me, I would let the Watch Commander know exactly what happened." Being on probation, I had this overwhelming pucker-factor feeling. However, I knew that integrity and honesty were the best policy, especially for me. It was not the end of the world, and I would survive this incident. However, if I lied, I would be terminated, and rightfully so!

After the suspect was logged into the holding tank at the station, Doyle and I entered the Watch Commander's office. At that point, I don't mind telling you I was scared shitless. Our Lieutenant, J. Rice, was Doyle's academy classmate. I stood before Lieutenant Rice at attention as Doyle stood behind me.

I cleared my throat and stated, "Sir, while taking our suspect into custody, I had an accidental discharge with the department's shotgun." Lieutenant Rice looked at me, smiled, and stated, "Did Jerry put you up to this?" Doyle peeked over my shoulder and replied, "Lieutenant, he had an accidental discharge with the shotgun while taking our armed suspect into custody."

At that point, the lieutenant's facial expression changed, and he directed Sergeant Lawson to respond to the scene and conduct a preliminary shooting investigation. Normally, Robbery Homicide Division would respond to all officer-involved shootings, except those shootings involving no "hits." Dog shootings, on the other hand, were usually handled at the divisional level. Sergeant Lawson completed his investigation, and I received two relinquished days for the shooting violation, meaning I would be working two of my regularly scheduled days off as punishment. I was good with that as opposed to being fired on probation. The lesson here was that telling the truth was not the end of the world. My honesty and integrity gave me credibility—and some additional shotgun remediation training!

LAPD Force Investigation Division
(Use of Deadly Force Protocol)

It was the policy of the Los Angeles Police Department that the Force Investigation Division (FID) investigates all incidents involving LAPD officers' use of deadly force resulting in a law enforcement-related injury (LERI). FID's Investigative responsibility also includes all deaths of the arrestees or detainees in the custodial care of the LAPD, accidental shootings, animal shootings and other investigations as directed by the Chief of Detectives. All uses of force are evaluated based on if the force used is objectively reasonable.

The term "reasonably necessary" has been replaced by the legal term "objectively reasonable. "The Los Angeles Police Department defined the legal standard used to determine the lawfulness and appropriateness of a use of force based on the Fourth Amendment to the United States Constitution, which protects people from unreasonable searches and seizures by government officials.

In Graham v. Connor (490 U.S. 386 [1989]), Graham stated in part, that the reasonableness of a particular use of force must be judged from the perspective of a reasonable officer on the scene, rather than with the 20/20 vision of hindsight.

Reasonableness must allow for the fact that police officers often must make split-second judgments—in circumstances that are intense, uncertain, and rapidly evolving—about the amount of force that is necessary in a particular situation. The test of reasonableness defies a precise definition or mechanical application. The force must be reasonable under the circumstances known to the officer at the time it is used. Therefore, the department examines all uses of force from an objective standard rather than a subjective standard.

Phase Two Probation (PM Watch)

I made it through phase one of my probationary training program with FTOs Doyle and Appleby. Now, it was time to move into phase two. I was assigned to PM watch, which was a lot busier than morning watch. There would be more people roaming the streets, more gangs and narcotics activity. I would be assigned to Unit 5A19, one of two Wilmington basic cars, and my new FTO was another seasoned veteran with over 25 years on the job who was also a business owner. He had a T-shirt shop in San Pedro and a check cashing business in the city of Torrance.

On more than one occasion when he arrived to work I could tell he was tired. All in all, he was a low-key FTO that handled his patrol area. On the nights he was off, I worked with a seasoned Police Officer II. That's when I really got a chance to do some police work. I remember during one roll call, we had a guest speaker from Narcotics Division, Detective Vincent. He told the entire roll call about this new street drug that was taking over communities. He identified the illegal substance as "cocaine in rock form." Although Detective Vincent spoke in great detail about the drug, he never provided us with any photographs that showed what it actually looked like.

Speaking of cocaine, I can remember engaging in foot pursuit on numerous occasions in the area of Wilmington Boulevard, Craven Avenue, and "F" Street chasing gang members. I can safely say that on at least a half dozen occasions, I would detain gang members, who would be sweating profusely with rapid heartbeats. When asked, "Why you so nervous homeboy? Are you carrying something illegal that I need to know about?" The standard response would be, "No sir. I'm clean officer." I would complete a field interview card (FI card) to document our stop and the type of activity involved. If they were not arrested, I would warn them about loitering in the area. More than once, I would chase a suspect through the projects before detaining them. Many times, I would observe several small off-white rocks on the sidewalk. At that point in my young career, I didn't have a clue what I was actually observing on the ground.

So, I would complete my investigation, which included running them for outstanding warrants and wants, before warning them about trespassing. I know the gangsters were probably laughing their butts off at this clueless probationary officer when I cleared the location.

Well, all that was about the change! One PM Watch, my partner and I received a radio call regarding possible gang activity in the Dana Strand Housing Projects, located in Wilmington. As my partner and I drove up to the location, a male suspect looked in our direction then took off running holding his waistband. I foot bailed out of the passenger's front seat of our police vehicle, and the foot pursuit was on. I gave my location to Communications Division as my partner paralleled me. I finally caught up with the suspect near Hawaiian Avenue and G Street after tackling him like a linebacker.

I noticed the suspect's right hand was still concealed inside his right front waistband area. Believing the suspect was attempting to arm himself, I quickly placed my two-inch Smith & Wesson .38 caliber revolver to the back of his head and whispered in his ear, "Hey stupid, if you fail to follow my instructions from this point on, you are leaving earth tonight in the dark. I want you to slowly pull your right hand out of your waistband and keep it in plain sight where I can see it. Do you understand?"

He complied and was handcuffed without further incident. When I conducted the pat down search of his right waistband area, I recovered a small clear cellophane zip lock baggie that contained approximately forty to fifty off-white rocks resembling, "cocaine in rock form." I looked at the suspect and stated, "This must be cocaine in rock form!" To my surprise, the suspect spontaneously stated, "Yes sir!" From that day forward, it was on like Donkey Kong! Especially now that I knew what cocaine in rock form looked like, the local gangsters and drug dealers were in trouble.

General Electric

(Taser Therapy)

Probation was going along well for me. My next FTO, Police Officer III Jeff Christ (JC), he was one of my favorite FTOs. JC had acquired the nickname "General Electric" because he believed in using the taser to de-escalate potentially violent situations. I referred to this as, "taser therapy." I recall working PM watch in Wilmington when JC and I received a radio call: "Burglary from motor vehicle (BFMV) suspect there now in the carport area of the Dana Strand Housing Projects." Upon our arrival, we observed the suspect, who saw us and climbed upon the carport roofing area. I requested additional units and set up a good perimeter, as JC continued to verbalize with the uncooperative suspect, who refused to climb down from the carport roof.

JC deployed the taser and pointed it at the suspect, who was ordered to drop the screwdriver he was holding. However, he continued to refuse JC's verbal commands. Since verbalization was ineffective, JC fired the taser. It struck the suspect in his upper torso and lower extremities causing him to drop the screwdriver, fall off the roof and land onto the ground below, all within seconds. Still somewhat uncooperative even after being tased, he refused to comply with our verbal commands to place his hands behind his back and to stop resisting. To overcome his bizarre and combative behavior, I deployed my PR-24 Baton and used a couple of power strokes to strike the suspect on his upper right arm and lower legs while ordering him to place his hands behind his back and stop resisting. It was like pure, freaking magic; the suspect got the message immediately, complied, and was taken into custody without any further incident. He received medical treatment and was OK to be booked for the BFMV.

I learned a lot from JC in terms of tactics, observation arrests, and narcotics. Soon, I would be rotated to Day Watch and assigned to work with FTO Police Officer III+I Wally Crane (WC). Now, being assigned to Day watch was far different than of my previous two watches. We dealt mainly with heroin addicts and a lot of residential burglaries. WC taught me how to identify and arrest addicts under the influence of heroin.

During Day Watch, heroin addicts roamed the streets looking for ways to get their next fix and were responsible for a lot of the daytime residential burglaries. WC and I handled different types of calls for service and even one felony marijuana arrest of a man in a jeep.

Jeep Wrangler & Marijuana

One sunny afternoon, WC and I were assigned to Unit 5A43, a San Pedro basic car. WC was driving and I was keeping books. We were headed northbound in the number one lane of traffic on Gaffey Street when I observed this black Jeep Wrangler being driven by a male White adult make a quick right turn onto Gaffey Street from 36th Street. All of a sudden, I saw a brick of what appeared to be marijuana fly out of the driver's side of the Jeep into traffic. The driver quickly pulled over to the east curb on Gaffey Street, exited the car, and retrieved the item of interest. After he placed it underneath the driver's seat, I alerted WC of my observation and told him I believed the suspect was in possession of a brick of marijuana.

We followed the vehicle northbound on Gaffey Street until 24th Street while requesting DMV and auto status of the suspect's vehicle. WC activated our forward-facing red light to conduct an investigative traffic stop. We both exited our police vehicle; WC became the designated cover officer and allowed me to approach the vehicle as the designated contact officer. As I approached the driver's side of the Jeep, my suspicions were confirmed. Sitting right there in plain view was a brick of marijuana wrapped in clear cellophane underneath the driver's seat of the Jeep. The suspect was taken into custody, his Jeep was impounded and the marijuana seized, weighed, packaged, and booked into evidence.

When I explained my observations to the watch commander while requesting booking approval, he laughed and said that was too easy. I responded, "Sir, I bet the suspect's defense attorney will cross examine me and say the same thing."

When the deployment period was over, I was assigned to another day watch FTO.

My next FTO was Police Officer III Don Jenks (DJ). RIP brother! I loved working with DJ; he was a no-nonsense, proactive police officer. There was no doubt in my mind that DJ would cite the president of the United States if he violated the rules of the road.

One early Sunday morning, DJ and I were working the streets of San Pedro. It was quiet. Some business owners were washing down the sidewalks in front of their businesses. We observed three young Black juveniles, all holding Bibles walking northbound on Pacific Avenue at 7th Street, as they entered the marked crosswalk with the "Don't walk" signal flashing. DJ, our car commander, stopped the trio and pulled out his citation book. He was poised to cite all three of them.

Normally, I would have no problem, but it was Sunday. I stepped up and asked DJ if I could speak with him privately before he started citing the juveniles. During our conversation, I begged him not to cite those kids. "Sir, listen. These are probably the nicest children in all of San Pedro. They all have Bibles in their hands, not guns or drugs. They are dressed in Sunday attire, not gang attire." DJ looked at me and said he would give them a verbal warning this time only. That made my day!

Proactive Policing

John Karle (JK) and Jim McDonnell (JM) were two Harbor Community police officers that I admired for the way they took care of business back in the day. JM was eventually promoted to the rank of Assistant Chief with LAPD, hired as Chief of Police with Long Beach Police Department, and voted in as the Sheriff of Los Angeles County. JK and JM represented the badge with pride, integrity, and guts. Their style of police work was inspirational for me, as a young police officer, to watch. They were unbiased and displayed a take-no-prisoners mentality.

Our badge said, "Police Officer–City of Los Angeles." I often told suspects that there was not a square inch of real estate within the city that I was afraid of. Were there dangerous areas? Oh hell yeah! We would just get back up and overwhelm our enemy with a show of force. When we detained gangsters for gang activity, I made it a point to tell them, "We're going to be here everyday and twice on Sundays! This is our city and the neighborhoods belong to the taxpayers, not gangsters."

One of my favorite pastimes was arresting gangsters on Fridays. While transporting them to the station, I would advise them that gang banging offered no benefits, no 401K, no future, no room for promotion, and there was definitely no pension or medical benefits for a life of crime. My philosophy was, "I'd give them twenty years, two days at a time, in jail." Booking gangsters for their outstanding warrants on Friday evening after business hours dramatically reduced the incidents of violent crime like drive-by shootings and homicides. Since courts were closed and serving time on the weekends was considered dead time, most of the arrestees would not appear in court until the following Tuesday when they would be granted time served or remanded to the custody of the Los Angeles County Sheriff's Department, Men's Central Jail.

Like every good police officer, when I dealt with a "gangster," I considered it my civic duty to remove their current arrest warrant from the system and also issue them another citation for the current violation because I knew from experience that they weren't going to take care of it in a timely manner. Thus, they got another free trip to the gray bar hotel, which offered them three hots and a cot!

I felt truly humbled that the Los Angeles Police Department had allowed me the distinct privilege of protecting and serving the citizens of Los Angeles. I took pride in relocating low-life predators who preyed upon innocent victims and suspects who sold illegal drugs to drug addicts within the community.

"We're going to be here everyday and twice on Sundays! This is our city and the neighborhood belongs to the taxpayers not gangsters."

During the eighties, rock cocaine destroyed a lot of families and negatively impacted the community. We would see—especially during morning watch—

zombies walking around; women so strung out and often involved in prostitution, selling their bodies for literally nothing just to support their rock cocaine addiction. It was truly a sad situation. Meanwhile, drug dealers were rolling. So, whenever I had an opportunity to seize their narcotics, money, firearms, and vehicles, I did so proudly. They did not care about the community, so I did not care about their illegal drug-dealing butts either.

CHAPTER 9

1984 Summer Olympic Games

One of the highlights of my career was working the 1984 Summer Olympic Games in the city of Los Angeles. The games of the 23rd Olympiad were held July 28 through August 12. We referred to it as the Sixteen Days of Summer. The LAPD was mobilized for approximately 33 days, which included regular patrol assignments and Olympic assignments. Crime within the 468 square miles patrolled by LAPD did not stop, so resources were divided. It was the second time in history that the city of Los Angeles had hosted the Olympic games. This was an international, multi-sport event, and policing it required major planning and law enforcement deployment. So imagine protecting over 6,829 athletes, approximately 5,263 men and 1,566 women, in addition to thousands of spectators. There were two main venues, Westwood and South Los Angeles. The south venue was located in Southwest Patrol Division at the Los Angeles Coliseum and Swim Stadium. The cities of Carson, Chino Hills, and Irvine also hosted some of the Games.

I was assigned to both Los Angeles venues. I remember we were bused into the South Bureau's Field Command Post (FCP) Lenicia B. Weems Elementary School, located at 1260 W. 36th Place in Los Angeles. We all worked 12-hour shifts. Each venue had perimeter security to monitor and protect the numerous resources stored at the locations. I recalled thinking, "What a BS assignment for 12 hours." Well, guess who got assigned to the 12-hour BS assignment at the FCP? Me!

During my shift, I volunteered to do food and logistical runs. If the Incident Commander needed some light bulbs, I would go and purchase them.

So, during my travels through Southwest Patrol Division, I was traveling northbound on Denker Avenue toward 39th Street. As I reached that intersection, I observed numerous gang members loitering. The situation made me think of our academy training, when we learned about different radio codes and destinations. One in particular was related to gang activity. If we needed additional units, all we had to do was broadcast that we were "Code 6 George." So, on this day, I did what any officer with my amount of time on the job would do. I advised Communications Division to show me Code 6 George at Denker Avenue and 39th Street where

I was monitoring several gang members. Numerous patrol units responded to my location. At least 10 units rolled up to investigate the gang activity. Several arrests were made for different health and safety and penal code violations. Soon after, I had to get back to my assigned duties at the FCP, but having the opportunity to hook up a couple of hardcore gang members made my day.

It was a totally different story, when I worked the West Venue. The freaking sidewalks rolled up by midnight in Westwood. There was nothing to do, but watch paint dry. There were no calls for service being broadcasted from Communications Division. We might see a pair of headlights moving down the street only to be disappointed because it was another patrol unit driving around, bored.

LAX Bomb Hoax

On the last day of the 23rd Olympics, an officer from Metropolitan Division and assigned to the LAX Protection Detail, notified Communications Division that he had discovered a destructive device, which he had allegedly defused. He had been awarded all sorts of honors, in addition to being credited for disarming the destructive device, which he had allegedly observed on a bus filled with luggage belonging to the Turkish Olympic Athletic Team. LAPD Investigators became somewhat suspicious of the officer's account of events due to numerous inconsistencies. After further investigation and interrogation, the officer admitted to planting the fake destructive device. Sadly criminal charges were filed against him, which resulted in his arrest. He was subsequently convicted, placed on five years probation, ordered to pay restitution in the amount of $10,000.00 and terminated.

Vandalism Suspect There Now

(Internal Affairs Complaint Investigation No. 84-1235)

The Olympics were over. I went back to day watch patrol in Harbor Patrol Division.

On December 4, 1984, I was deployed as Unit 5U1, a (one officer) report car. Basically, your job as a report car was to respond to calls for service. For example, there was a STROM log located in the Watch Commander's office listing persons who needed reports taken for crimes, like theft from motor vehicles, residential burglaries, vandalisms, etc.

On a nice sunny afternoon, after I had just taken a crime report in the northern section of Harbor Patrol Division in an area referred to as "The Strip," Communications Division broadcast: "Any Harbor Unit, handle this call first. Vandalism suspect there now. PR states the suspect was puncturing the tires on his vehicle parked in his front yard. The suspect was described as a male, Hispanic, wearing blue jeans, a white long-sleeve shirt, dark baseball cap, and moustache, armed with a screwdriver. Your call is Code 2."

I responded to the call for service within minutes of it being broadcast and showed myself Code 6 at the location. In fact, I could still hear the air seeping out of the victim's tires. According to the victim, the suspect was last seen on-foot, walking northbound on Halldale Avenue from 207th Street. I had the victim get into the front seat of my patrol vehicle to see if we could locate the suspect. Since it was a misdemeanor not committed in my presence, the victim would have to place the suspect under citizen arrest verbally.

As we drove around the corner, I observed the suspect matching the description walking westbound on the south side of 206th Street. I advised Communications Division I was Code 6 on a possible vandalism suspect and requested an additional unit to my location. Within 30 seconds, here comes Good Ole Sarge. I had taken an position of advantage behind the driver's door of my police vehicle armed with my department firearm in the low-ready position. I ordered the suspect to place his arms above his head and to turn around slowly. My main concern was to check his waistband area to see if he was still armed with the screwdriver.

In the meantime, Good Ole Sarge looked in my direction and gave me the thumbs-up signal, so I thought he was going to be the designated cover officer. I left my position of advantage to approach and conduct a pat-down search of the suspect before placing him into custody. Suddenly, the suspect decided to turn toward me. I immediately responded to his aggressive behavior and refusal to follow my verbal commands by forcing him onto the ground to handcuff him.

Well, Good Ole Sarge finally left his cover position and ordered me to take the handcuffs off and to immediately release the suspect. Good Ole Sarge further advised me that we were not going to arrest the positively identified vandalism suspect. I was wondering, what's up with that? I'm a new police officer with just over one year of experience, but this didn't smell right. Good Ole Sarge ordered me to meet him back at the station. So, I took the victim back to his residence and completed the crime report listing the person I had detained as the primary suspect.

According to department policy, if you were involved in a Use of Force Incident with no arrest, you were required to complete a Use of Force Face Sheet, Form 1.67.2 and 15.7 narrative, to document the incident.

It was a good thing I knew the department's policy because Good Ole Sarge's intent was to burn me. I would learn later that there was a Sergeant II position vacancy that had been advertised for Harbor Patrol Division. So, I can only imagine Good Ole Sarge wanted to show our Area Harbor commanding officers that he had no problem initiating a 1.81 Personnel Complaint Investigation against an officer, particularly me. He would complete the fact sheet and allege that I used unauthorized tactics and force. I provided my interview along after completing a detailed description summary of my actions and verbally articulated why I took the actions I did on that particular day.

The lesson learned here was anytime a supervisor rolled up to your scene, never expect them to get involved. Their job was to supervise, monitor, coach, guide, and direct. However, in this case, Good Ole Sarge thought his job was to screw me over for the sake of his own personal gain! Before the complaint was adjudicated, I was transferred out to Pacific Patrol Division.

Commendations Harbor Patrol Division

11/07/1984	COMMENDATION
Officer Landrum you are commended for your concern, attention to duty and gentleness during a difficult molestation investigation involving a young female victim.	
11/14/1984	COMMENDATION
Officer Landrum you are commended by the School Principal for being helpful, courteous, considerate and professional while helping with a molestation situation involving an elementary student, who had been molested by her stepfather.	

CHAPTER 10

Pacific Community Police Station

(Aka Pacific Patrol Division)

O n December 9, 1984, while awaiting the Harbor Patrol Division complaint to be adjudicated, I was officially transferred to Pacific Patrol Division referred to as Pacific Community Police Station. It was the home of the world famous Venice Beach and the Los Angeles World International Airport (LAX). Pacific Division was the second-most visited place in California, with Disneyland ranking number one. LAX was one of the busiest airports in the United States. The Pacific Community was approximately 25.74 square miles with approximately 200,000 residents. Pacific Patrol Division provided police services to the neighborhoods of Venice Beach, Oakwood, Mar Vista, Playa del Rey, Playa Vista, Palms, and Westchester.

Pacific Area Reporting District Map

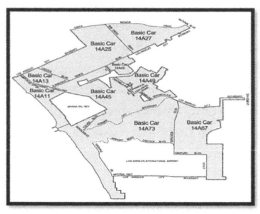

Personnel Complaint Adjudication

One afternoon while working, I received a radio call to respond to the station. Upon my arrival, the Watch Commander advised me that the Patrol Commanding Officer wanted to meet with me. I responded to the area office and met with Captain I Ron Banks, who had received and reviewed the complaint investigation initiated while I was assigned to Harbor Patrol Division, and it was time for adjudication.

I listened intently as Captain Banks read over the allegations, which were identified as one count of unauthorized force and one count of unauthorized tactics. Captain Banks advised me that based on the circumstances; the complaint against me was going to be exonerated.

Now, I was clueless, so I asked Captain Banks what the term, "exonerated" meant. Back then I had no idea. Captain Banks responded, "Well, it means that everything you did on the day of the complaint involving the suspect was proper, lawful, and justified." I signed off on the complaint adjudication and thought to myself, Good Ole Sarge wasted valuable man-hours on a frivolous complaint investigation. The story had a happy ending; he was not selected for the Sergeant II position. I'm glad someone else besides me noted he was a buffoon, who lacked good judgment and common sense!

Special Problems Unit

It did not take long before Pacific Patrol Division's Area Commanding Officer, Captain Mills, authorized the deployment of Pacific Division's Special Problems Unit (SPU) to combat and suppress street crime within the division. Coincidentally, Wilshire Police Division was experiencing a rash of bank robberies during the same time period. During one deployment period, our SPU Team was loaned to Wilshire Patrol Division for crime suppression. My new partner was Police Officer II Keith Lewis, who was one of my best radio call partners, as well as, a good friend during my tenure with the Los Angeles Police Department and also in retirement.

Sergeant I Kenneth Hillman was our direct supervisor. For the entire deployment period, we would patrol the streets of Wilshire Patrol Division and focus on crime suppression. The Commanding Officers for Wilshire Patrol Division during that time period were Captains Bivens and Washington.

During our first day, after sitting through a long roll call orientation regarding the crime issues that plagued Wilshire Patrol Division, Keith and I cleared the station, motivated and ready to get in the mix. Keith was the senior car commander, since he was from Class 12/82. I used to joke with him by saying, "Wow, you have a whole five months more time on the job than me. You're a real seasoned veteran!" Keith and I were not entirely certain of the southern boundaries for Wilshire Patrol Division or where Southwest Patrol Division's boundaries began. I recall Keith driving southbound on Western Avenue toward Adams Boulevard. Suddenly, we were flagged down by a citizen, who stated, there was a man robbing the Chevron gas station on the southeast corner of Western Avenue at Adams Boulevard. Keith and I felt like "Johnny on the Spot." No sooner had I broadcasted our Code 6 location, the suspect emerged from the convenience store, looked in our direction, and took off running in a southeast direction through a fenced-in parking lot adjacent to the Chevron gas station. Keith and I followed homeboy and decided to patiently wait for him to realize he was fenced in. Once knucklehead realized what was happening, he thought it would be a good idea to make an attempt to run through Keith and I. Well that didn't work out too well for him! I used my PR-24 baton and generated a well-deserved power stroke to his lower left leg. Knucklehead dropped like a sack of potatoes and was taken into custody without any further incident. Our investigation disclosed the suspect was actually a petty theft suspect, who had stolen several packs of cigarettes.

Duty to Report Use of Force Incidents

Anytime, you were involved in a use-of-force incident, your immediate supervisor or the first supervisor to respond had to be made aware of your involvement. In this particular case, I requested Sergeant Hillman and notified him. The suspect received medical treatment and was given an OK to be booked at

Parker Center Jail, which we referred to as, "The Glass House." We also learned that Western Avenue at Adams Boulevard was actually Southwest Patrol Division's Jurisdiction.

Keith and I would continue to make several arrests throughout the deployment period for narcotics and other criminal offenses. Finally, the deployment period was over, and we were headed back to Pacific Patrol Division. Adjacent to Venice Beach was a small neighborhood community known as, "Oakwood" where there were a couple of hot spots for gang and narcotics activity: 1002 5th Avenue, 410 Indiana Avenue, and 632 Vernon Avenue.

There were Black and Hispanic Street gangs living within those areas. Cocaine in rock form and marijuana were the drugs of choice. Although, heroin was prevalent, cocaine was the issue. Keith and I made arrests daily for California Health and Safety Code §11350(a), possession of a controlled substance resembling cocaine in rock form, which was a felony then. We would also arrest knuckleheads for California Health and Safety Code §11351.5 and 11352, possession, sales and transportation of controlled substances resembling cocaine in rock form. We made numerous arrests of gangsters in possession of loaded firearms as well.

Marionwood Housing Development Projects

Approximately, one mile from Pacific Patrol Station was the Marionwood Housing Development Projects on Inglewood Avenue at Marionwood Drive. One thing I recalled during my tour of duty at Pacific Patrol Division was every time a shots-fired call came out in the Marionwood Housing Projects, it was a good shooting (unfortunately). I'm not talking about shots just being fired; I'm talking about a body down with multiple gunshot wounds. For a while, I was called the Angel of Death because I would detain gang members who were loitering and did not live in the Marionwood Housing Projects. It was obvious they were involved in some type of nefarious activity. I would warn them of arrests and about the area being notorious for shootings. Why would they not adhere to sound advice from a police officer? Mainly because they were felony stupid, selling illegal narcotics and did not give a damn about the police! After the verbal warning, we would clear the location and sometime during the shift, we would get the "shots fired" call, respond, and locate the same subject whom I had warned earlier, fatally shot—DRT or dead right there.

Now this might sound a little cold hearted, but we would classify such a shooting incident as NHI (no human involvement). It eliminated two problems plaguing the community: a drug dealer/gangster plus the outstanding murder suspect!

Street Justice

From time to time, we would respond to calls for service involving "street justice." For instance, I responded to a burglary from a motor vehicle suspect being detained by citizens in Marionwood. This particular suspect was overly happy to see us upon our arrival.

My partner and I should have been awarded the prestigious Medal of Valor for saving his life. Those victims beat the sugar, honey, and ice tea out of him. We requested a supervisor and the Los Angeles City Fire Paramedics to render first aid and to ensure that the suspect told what really happened to him. I never saw a suspect so happy to be in police custody and willing to go to jail for his safety.

Pacific Patrol Division had its share of liberal residents, too; those who felt they were above the law. For example, anytime we conducted enforcement activity on Venice Beach, it would result in an anti-police response. So, we had to be smarter than them. They felt that smoking marijuana and using cocaine in public view was perfectly normal. They also felt the laws and constitution did not apply to them. So, every opportunity I, and many others like me had, we would enforce the letter of the law, as opposed to the spirit of the law, just to remind them that there were consequences for breaking the law. Venice Beach was its own three-ring circus, especially on the weekends.

There were three popular nightspots within Pacific Patrol Division: Popcorn's, TGI Fridays, and Chippendales. Popcorn's and TGI Fridays were both centrally located near the intersections of Lincoln Boulevard and Maxella Avenue just north of the 90 Marina Freeway. Chippendales was located on Motor Avenue north of Venice Boulevard.

Usually on Friday and Saturday nights, we would be dressed in our Class A uniforms, long sleeve shirt, and traditional black clip-on ties. Uniform inspections were usually held on Fridays to ensure our shoes did not look like we shined them with a Hershey's chocolate bar, our duty weapon were clean and loaded with department-approved ammunition, and our leather gear and overall uniform appearance was professional.

I worked with a group of police officers that took pride in being professional. We qualified weekly at the Academy's Bonus Firearm Range to maintain our marksmanship. In any event, Friday and Saturday nights belonged to us. During this time, most of us were single, so whenever the Los Angeles City Fire Marshall requested police assistance at Chippendales, we would set new land speed records to get there. Just having the opportunity to see a bunch of beautiful women all gathered in one place, as opposed to being on a crime scene was outstanding.

I heard that some of my colleagues would get lucky and procure a phone number. I just stood by to enjoy the scenery because I knew after we cleared; it was back to normal patrol. During my tenure with Keith, we made numerous arrests, received numerous commendations and even got involved in an officer-involved shooting while off duty in Southeast Patrol Division, aka Watts.

CHAPTER 11

Off-Duty Officer- Involved Shooting

(Watts, California)

On Tuesday, December 17, 1985, Keith and I had just finished working out at Pacific Patrol Division's gym. We had carpooled to work that particular day. My former fiancé's parents lived on 112th Street east of Compton Avenue in Watts. Earlier in the day, she had her wisdom teeth extracted and decided to stay overnight at her parent's home. So, I decided to stop by to check on her and see if she needed anything. In the meantime, Keith and I were hungry. By the time we had driven from Marina Del Rey to Watts, we were starving. There was a Kentucky Fried Chicken located on the northeast corner of Compton Avenue at Imperial Highway. I recalled Keith and I pulling into the drive-through to place our order. We were waiting in line, approximately four vehicles back from the drive through order window. Meanwhile, we observed this yellow Pontiac LeMans occupied by two male, White adults drive into the KFC's parking lot and parked on the eastside, out of our view.

The next thing, Keith and I observe are two male, Black adults riding on a beach cruiser diagonally crossing the intersection of Imperial Highway at Compton Avenue in a northwesterly direction. The passenger seated on the handlebars pulled out a handgun and started shooting at a male, Black adult wearing what appeared to be a maroon sweat suit with a white strip running down the sides of his sweat pants.

We observed the victim fall to the pavement, quickly get back up to his feet and run away southbound out of view with an obvious limp. Keith and I immediately exited his vehicle and took cover behind a yellow Volvo parked in the KFC parking lot. Keith and I were armed with our five-shot Smith & Wesson .38 caliber revolvers with two speedy loaders. As the suspects rode on the west side of Compton Avenue north of Imperial Highway attempting to enter the Nickerson Gardens housing projects, Keith and I identified ourselves as Los Angeles Police Officers. I recall ordering the suspect on the handlebars to drop his weapon and get on the ground. Instead, he pointed his gun in our direction. Based on the totality of the circumstances, an immediate defense of life situation, an officer-involved shooting (OIS) occurred. I fired my off-duty weapon at the fleeing suspect.

Although my actions to the reader may seem like a split-second decision, Los Angeles Police Officers are well trained to consider two critical factors when using deadly force. Those critical factors consisted of two acronyms: IDOL (imminent defense of life) and BALKS (background, age, last resort, knowledge of crime, and seriousness of crime). The suspect in this case had taken actions that necessitated the Use of Deadly Force. He was armed, dangerous, and had already fired numerous rounds at the victim. During the OIS, the two male, White adults we had observed earlier walked up behind Keith and I both wearing trench coats. One of them was holding a brick L.A. cellular telephone.

Keith and I identified ourselves as Los Angeles Police Officers and directed them to call 9-1-1. I told them to tell the emergency operator that two off-duty Los Angeles Police Officers, not in uniform, had just been involved in an officer-involved-shooting. This was a fast-moving and fluid situation that could have gone south quickly.

As Southeast Patrol Units responded to our location, the two male, White adults identified themselves to me as bail enforcement agents. One of them turned out to be a key witness; he recalled the shooting and told investigators that the suspect had pulled the trigger when pointing the gun in our direction.

Just prior to units arriving, Keith and I moved toward the location where I fired my weapon.

Based on the geographical area and totality of the circumstances, Keith and I decided it was in our best interest to recover the suspect's firearm, which he dropped during my OIS. The second suspects had abandoned the beach cruiser, which was lying on the ground in a dirt field north of the OIS location and near the east entrance into the Nickerson Gardens Housing Projects.

I vividly recall Police Officer II Jeff Zych being one of the first uniformed officers to respond to our location. I knew Jeff from our Harbor Patrol Division days. I provided him with my public safety statement, which basically stated that the suspect was armed and, I was the involved shooter, I fired one round in a westerly direction at the armed suspect. The statement also included a description of the suspect and his clothing, as well as, his last known direction of travel.

Shortly after Jeff arrived to our call for "Help," numerous other department resources began to arrive, including the Southeast Patrol Division's Assistant Watch Commander (AWC). Initially, it appeared that he did not believe what had occurred—I could tell by that Bullshit look on his face. I was pissed. We had no reason to lie or make up anything.

This was a righteous officer-involved shooting. I recommended that someone contact Detective Headquarters Division and have them put out a medical alert to all the local hospitals in the event that our victim/suspect showed up to be treated for gunshot wounds. Approximately 15 to 20 minutes later, Martin Luther King Drew Medical Center notified Southeast Patrol Division that they had a victim of a shooting walk into their emergency room.

I remember asking the AWC to find out from the medical personnel what the person was wearing. When they told us the person was wearing a maroon sweat suit with a white stripe and had sustained a gunshot wound to the lower leg, I responded by saying, "Do you believe me now, sir?"

Robbery Homicide Division

Robbery Homicide Division had been notified and was en route to conduct their shooting investigation, which included interviewing all witnesses, as well as, Keith and me. In the meantime, we were transported to Southeast Patrol Division to be interviewed.

Beach Cruiser Stolen

An officer was assigned to the crime scene. He had one job that night: protect the crime scene, which included the outstanding suspect's beach cruiser. You can't make this stuff up; someone was able to steal the beach cruiser from the crime scene while Keith and I were being interviewed at the station. I am not sure what occurred, but really! The beach cruiser was stolen from the crime scene.

Robbery Crime Broadcast

The next morning; Keith and I had a court appearance in West Los Angeles from an unrelated arrest we made months earlier. We had driven to Pacific Patrol Division, checked out a dual-purpose patrol vehicle, and drove to the West Los Angeles County Superior Court at 1633 Purdue Avenue. Our court case concluded around 1130 hours, and while returning to the station, we over-heard a radio call regarding an armed robbery in-progress at the McDonalds Restaurant on National and Sawtelle boulevards. Keith and I were less than a half-block away.

We went Code 6 and determined that the suspects had fled. I told Keith, the department would have had a baby if the suspect(s) had been at the scene and we had gotten into another officer-involved shooting. Keith looked at me, smiled, and said, "Well, Buzz, they would get over it!"

Use of Force Review Board Adjudication

(Officer-Involved Shooting Investigation No. 173)

The department's Use of Force Review Board convened several months after the shooting to adjudicate the actions of Keith and me. According to the UOF Review Board, on the evening of December 17, 1985, our tactics were appropriate, the drawing of our weapons and my use of deadly force were ruled all in-policy.

CHAPTER 12
California Felony Murder Rule

I n 1984, the state of California charged defendants involved in the commission of a felonious crime that resulted in a death with murder based on California's felony murder rule, aka the vicarious murder rule. For example, suspects A and B decide to commit a vehicle burglary. During the commission of that vehicle burglary, Suspect A is shot and killed by the victim during the commission of the crime. Although Suspect A was killed, the victim would not likely face murder charges depending on the totality of the circumstances. However, Suspect B, a participant in the vehicle burglary, would most likely be charged with the shooting death of Suspect A. Sounds like something that happens in a Hollywood movie, right?

Well, hold on a minute: The factual caper that I am about to describe became a real eye opener for my partner, Police Officer II Andy Blanch and me. We were assigned to PM watch at Pacific Patrol Division, working Unit 14A67, when we received the below listed radio broadcast from Communications Division.

"14A67, 14A67, handle this call first. Meet Inglewood PD at Daniel Freeman Hospital, Inglewood holding two juvenile murder suspects in custody. Your call is Code 2."

Andy and I responded to the hospital and were met by our Pacific Area Homicide Detective Coordinator, who advised us that the two juveniles being detained were involved in an attempted burglary from motor vehicle somewhere in the Westchester area earlier in the evening and were confronted by the vehicle's owner, who shot and killed their juvenile friend.

After the decedent was shot, our two juveniles placed his body in their vehicle and drove him to Daniel Freeman Hospital emergency room for medical treatment. Whenever anyone is shot, hospitals are required to notify local law enforcement. In this case, Daniel Freeman Hospital contacted their local law enforcement agency, Inglewood Police Department.

Follow-Up Investigation

The two juveniles were placed into custody and escorted to our black and white police vehicle to be transported to Pacific Patrol Division. At the direction of the Officer-in-Charge of Pacific Division Homicide, who was following us, we were directed to drive the juveniles back to the Westchester area, in an effort to locate the original crime scene.

It should be duly noted that the actual shooter NEVER notified the Los Angeles Police Department that he had shot the juvenile and later discarded his firearm. In fact, he didn't even report the attempted burglary of his vehicle.

The juveniles were read their Miranda rights and described the suspect as a White male adult with short hair and facial hair. According to the juveniles, the suspect had exited from the back of a tractor-trailer parked near a vacant lot armed with an unknown type and caliber handgun just before he shot their friend.

Crime Scene Located

Meanwhile, Andy and I continued to canvass the general area and located a tractor-trailer parked near St. Bernard High School on St. Bernard Street. We noted that the back of the trailer had a single door on it. We informed Communications Division that we were Code 6 in the 7700 block of St Bernard Street with homicide detectives and would be knocking on the trailer door in search of a murder suspect.

Andy and I announced our presence and ordered everyone inside the trailer to exit with his or her hands in plain view. Within minutes, a male, White adult wearing a pair of jeans and white T-shirt with facial hair emerged from the rear door of the trailer with both hands in plain view as ordered. I was the designated contact officer while Andy was the designated cover officer. We took the suspect, who appeared to have a disabled left arm, into custody without incident.

Live-Field Show Up

The two juveniles positively identified him as the suspect during what was known as a live-field show up after being properly admonished. The Homicide OIC transported the male White adult to the station, while Andy and I transported the two juveniles to the station to be interviewed by homicide detectives. After a couple of hours, Andy and I were directed to book the juveniles for the murder of their friend under the vicarious murder rule.

According to the Homicide OIC, the shooter exited his living quarters armed with his revolver and confronted the suspects. During that confrontation, he fired one shot in fear of his life. The round struck one juvenile in his upper torso. Meanwhile, the other two juveniles panicked while attempting to put the decedent inside their car. They were not familiar with the area, so they drove to the nearest hospital, which turned out to be Daniel Freeman Hospital in Inglewood.

Immediately after the shooting, the alleged victim/shooter drove away from the crime scene, discarded the murder weapon and never notified the police.

According to the Homicide OIC, even thought the victim/shooter made no attempt to contact the police after shooting the decedent and got rid of the firearm used to shoot the juvenile, it was still a justifiable homicide, and the juveniles were being booked for one count each of 602 WIC 187 (a) P.C. under the California Felony Murder Rule.

As a young police officer, that blew my mind. Andy and I were never subpoenaed in this case, and I do not have any knowledge about how the murder case was adjudicated against the juveniles. Justice or injustice, all I know is that Andy and I did our job on that unfortunate night. The bottom line, it was a horrible night for everyone involved!

Commendations
Pacific Patrol Division

02/22/1985	LAFD LETTER OF APPRECIATION
Officer Landrum you are to be commended by LAFD for maintaining the peace during an emergency evacuation at the Popcorn's Night Club, which involved approximately 1,050 patrons.	
05/17/1985	COMMENDATION
Officer Landrum you are to be commended for attention to duty, investigative and interrogation techniques that led to the arrest of two robbery suspects, who cleared six other robberies.	
05/26/1985	COMMENDATION
Officer Landrum you are to be commended for your powers of observation, tactics and attention to duty, report writing abilities and interrogation techniques that led to incriminating statements and a felony filing against the suspect.	
08/26/1985	COMMENDATION
Officer Landrum you are to be commended for excellent interrogation techniques that gained the confidence of a PCP suspect that led to the filings of eight residential burglaries and 18 other burglaries.	
08/30/1985	COMMENDATION
Officer Landrum you are to be commended for attention to duty, knowledge of criminal element and powers of observation that led to arrest of a suspect described during roll call. Good police work!	
09/10/1985	COMMENDATION
Officer Landrum you are to be commended for your excellent tactics in response and deployment, physical and mental restraint in arresting a violent suspect without serious injury to self or others.	

10/19/1985	COMMENDATION

Officer Landrum you are to be commended for making a good narcotics arrest, excellent investigation and reports incorporating everything required to file felony charges.

12/04/1985	MAJOR COMMENDATION AWARD

Officer Landrum you are to be commended for your outstanding observations, knowledge of criminals in the area that led to arrest and criminal filing on vicious murder suspect where the victim was shot multiple times.

12/10/1985	COMMENDATION

Officer Landrum you are to be commended for conducting a quality investigation, observation and recovery of both a loaded gun and narcotics, as well as, the subsequent arrest of the parolee for armed robbery.

CHAPTER 13

West Bureau CRASH

(Community Resources Against Street Hoodlums)

On March 2, 1986, I was transferred to the West Bureau CRASH Gang Unit. The acronym CRASH stood for Community Resources Against Street Hoodlums. CRASH was considered a specialized operating unit within the Los Angeles Police Department deployed to combat gang-related crimes. CRASH was operational department-wide from 1979 to 2000. Being assigned to West Bureau CRASH provided me the opportunity to work any of the four geographical patrol divisions within West Bureau: Pacific Patrol Division, West Los Angeles Patrol Division, Hollywood Patrol Division and Wilshire Patrol Division.

Whatever division was experiencing major gang activity was where our gang unit would be assigned to patrol on any given tour of duty. West Bureau CRASH also had detectives and detective trainees assigned. CRASH units citywide handled gang-related crimes—assaults, robberies, shootings, homicides, etc. My partner was Police Officer II Rod Rodriguez, an outstanding street gang police officer and investigator.

Rod's vast knowledge and experience of the local street gangs in our area, as well as, his pro-aggressive style of police work was a perfect fit for me. We had a no-nonsense approach when it came to dealing with gangsters. Rod showed me the different gang territories within West Bureau. He embodied a true West Bureau CRASH officer.

91

Being assigned to West Bureau CRASH meant we were expected to be in top physical shape and condition. We trained daily and ran a couple of miles as a group from time-to-time. Our uniform and personal appearance was expected to be immaculate at all times, and we were also expected to qualify with our department firearm every week at the Academy during the bonus range qualification to maintain our marksmanship.

Gang-Related Murder – Hollywood Patrol Division

We usually worked Wilshire Patrol Division because of the ongoing street gang activity there. I recall one Friday night when Rod and I were assigned to Wilshire Division; we were hooking, booking and family cooking. It seemed like every investigative stop that night resulted in someone being hooked up.

In other words, we were proactively conducting investigative and consensual encounter enforcement stops with known gang members. One night, we had about four arrests from four different investigative stops. We were on our way to Wilshire Patrol Division to book our suspects, evidence and complete the necessary reports. Upon our arrival, while logging in our detained juveniles and adults, we received a Code Alpha meet in Wilshire Detectives.

We were advised that a gang-related homicide had just occurred in Hollywood Patrol Division at the intersection of Santa Monica Boulevard and Highland Avenue. The street gangs involved were identified as, "The Wanderers and The Drifters." It sounded like something out of a Hollywood movie, except this was real; a real person had been shot in the head and murdered during a confrontation with rival gang members. Rod and I scrambled to make notifications, to have the juveniles in our custody booked and cited out to their parents within the mandatory timeframe. The adults were a little easier to process. They were booked into the jail at Wilshire Station and housed there until they could post bail or were transferred to the Men's Central Jail controlled by the Los Angeles County Sheriff's Department.

Thankfully, the Wilshire Watch Commander on that particular night assigned a desk officer to assist Rod and I with all of our arrestees. They contacted the juvenile's parents. In the meantime, Rod and I responded to the Hollywood Division crime scene with our other colleagues.

I remember writing arrest reports while at the crime scene. The narcotics evidence seized had been secured in the evidence locker at Wilshire Patrol Division until we were available to return to weigh, seal, package and book it into evidence. In the meantime, our CRASH detectives were called to the crime scene. Murder was considered the ultimate crime, so when it came to pursuing murder suspects, there were no stones left unturned. All resources—and I mean all resources—were used to actively pursue and bring those responsible to justice.

This particular murder investigation was going to be a marathon. It was my first gang-related homicide with West Bureau CRASH. The detectives conducted their on-scene investigation, which included, canvassing the crime scene for evidence, measurements and photographs; identifying and interviewing witnesses; booking evidence; and notifying the Los Angeles County Coroner's Office to procure a Coroner's Case Number and arrange transportation of the decedent. Detectives contacted the Los Angeles Police Department's Scientific Investigation Division (SID) Photography Unit to photograph the crime scene.

The decedent's body was removed and the hunt was on for our outstanding murder suspect and the weapon. The follow-up investigation took us clear out to Valley Bureau, Foothill Patrol Division's area. Our detectives had uncovered information regarding the shooter and his identity. A Search and Probable Cause Arrest Warrant had been prepared to search the suspect's residence and for his arrest. Both warrants were endorsed for nighttime service, which meant, basically, that we could serve the warrants at any time of the day or night due to the serious and dangerous nature of the crime. That's right everyone; we made house calls often! Our attitude was, "We have guns, ammo, city car, city gas, and willing to travel to the ends of the earth to hook up a murder suspect!" You want to talk about an adrenaline rush! That's how it felt being a part of the entry and arrest team going after a verified murder suspect.

Remember that the suspect committed the ultimate crime, homicide. Such a predator is a danger to the community, and it was our job to locate and arrest him. Everything was predicated on the actions of the suspect. If he or she was cooperative, they were taken into custody without incident. If they decided not to cooperate, well shame on them!

"City car, city gas, guns, plenty of ammo, willing to travel to the ends of the earth to hook up a murder suspect!"

As a young police officer, I always wanted to either be the first or second entry team member through the door during house calls (search warrants). Tactics were a big deal, and LAPD taught us well, especially how to conduct crisis entries during search and arrest warrants. We trained all the time and would debrief about our tactical entries to see how we could improve for the next one.

Safety was the name of the game, and it has always been about officer survival while working the streets. We executed the search warrant service, and the suspect was gone. Detectives located and seized evidence that associated the outstanding murder suspect with his street gang. They interviewed his family members and gained some valuable information.

We cleared the location and debriefed the search warrant service over breakfast at the IHOP located at 7006 Hollywood Boulevard, across the street from Hollywood High School. I could hardly keep my eyes open; we were now going on 18 hours straight in our attempt to locate the outstanding murder suspect.

In the meantime, Rod and I still had to go back to Wilshire Patrol Division to complete our arrest and evidence reports and get them approved to book our evidence. Detectives continued their investigation, filed the case and disseminated a wanted suspect bulletin for the outstanding murder suspect, who was eventually located and arrested.

Unauthorized Force–Neglect of Duty

(Internal Affairs Complaint Investigation No. 86-0586)

While assigned to West Bureau CRASH, my assigned partner, Rod Rodriguez went on his scheduled vacation in deployment period No. 5. During his absence, I was assigned to work with another officer assigned to the unit. On May 4, 1986, we were assigned to work Wilshire Patrol Division. While conducting gang crime suppression, we stopped several gangsters on Redondo Avenue and Smiley Drive. As the designated contact officer, I proceeded to search one of the suspects, who had tried to evade us. I ordered him to spread his legs a part, so I could safely conduct a pat down search of his person for weapons and contraband based on his evasive and bizarre behavior.

He ignored my repeated verbal commands to spread his legs a part, so I used my left foot to spread his right leg. I completed the pat down search and placed him into custody for several outstanding arrest warrants. When we got to the station, I wrote the arrest report to describe how the suspect was linked to the numerous outstanding arrest warrants discovered under his alias names (The court does not do its own investigation; so it is up to the arresting officers to explain the nexus). In the meantime, as is customary, I had my partner review the report for accuracy before I submitted it for approval. The purpose of having a partner read the report is to check for grammatical errors and to ensure that the facts are correct. The report was reviewed, submitted, and approved.

The next day, I arrived for work and one of our sergeants advised me that I was being reassigned to work detectives. Sarge disclosed that there had been a personnel complaint initiated against me. I was completely in the dark; however, I noticed that my partner could not look me in the eyes. I wasn't exactly sure what was happening, but it did not take me long to figure out that my partner had something to do with it—bless her little heart!

Several days later, Sarge interviewed me about the detention and arrest of a gangster during our enforcement deployment in Wilshire Patrol Division. I explained the scope and nature of our investigative stop, and the subsequent arrest report. That's when Sarge told me the department was alleging that while on duty, I used unauthorized force against the suspect, when I kicked his right ankle apart during the pat down search. He also advised me that the department was also alleging that, while on duty, I neglected my duty when I failed to notify the department about the use of force. I explained my version of what occurred and how the suspect was uncooperative.

Furthermore, the suspect was not injured nor did he complain of injury to me on the night of his arrest. Sarge explained that my actions constituted a reportable use of force even though the suspect did not complain and I did not think it was a reportable use of force. I would learn later that the real motivation behind the complaint investigation involved a vacant Police Officer III position, which had become available within West Bureau CRASH. Normally, officers assigned to West Bureau CRASH were selected to fill the vacancy. Up until the surprise complaint, I felt good about my chances of being promoted.

During those days, the process for becoming a Field Training Officer involved taking a written examination, package review, and oral interview. There were three rankings: Outstanding, Excellent, and Good. I was listed on the eligibility list in the outstanding pool of available candidates for the position. My partner was also on the eligibility list as well. However, I was running circles around her work productivity when it came to proactive enforcement and monthly recap. So, I imagine she felt it would benefit her to initiate the personnel complaint against me. There is an old LAPD saying, "Burn them to learn them!" Well the fire in the furnace was warming up!

Complaint Investigation Adjudication
(Internal Affairs Complaint Investigation No. 86-0586)

The complaint allegations against me were all sustained, and I received seven-days on suspension. During my Skelly Hearing and adjudication, I respectfully requested to be transferred to Southwest Patrol Division. In hindsight, it was the right thing to do for all parties involved. Thanks Sarge!

Commendations
Operations-West Bureau CRASH

04/16/1986	COMMENDATION
Officer Landrum you are to be commended for job knowledge, attention to duty and outstanding tactics that led to the arrest of a Rollin 60 gang member in possession of a firearm.	
06/19/1986	COMMENDATION
Officer Landrum you are to be commended for powers of observation, attention to duty and outstanding "L" car tactics.	
07/07/1986	COMMENDATION
Officer Landrum you are to be commended for your outstanding teamwork, tactics and judgment during high-stress incident with armed suspects. Command presence, professional demeanor and good job arresting the suspects.	
07/24/1986	COMMENDATION
Officer Landrum you are to be commended for your dedication and perservance while doing an outstanding job.	
08/08/1986	COMMENDATION
Officer Landrum you are to be commended by the Reserve Corps Coordinator for your participation in firearm tactics training day for line and technical reserve officers.	

CHAPTER 14

Welcome to the Wild Southwest

Southwest Community Police Station

O n Sunday, August 17, 1986, I was officially transferred into Southwest Patrol Division, now referred to as Southwest Community Police Station. Welcome to the Wild Southwest. I was still a Police Officer II or "P2 Dawg" picking up the pieces from my untimely transfer from West Bureau CRASH. In any event, it was time to continue marching and establish my roots in the Wild Southwest. I was immediately assigned to PM Watch as Unit 3U1, which was basically, a one-officer report car. It didn't matter to me where I was assigned as long as I was working in the field. For me, it was a win-win situation. I knew my worth; I was just waiting for my chance to showcase my knowledge, skills and abilities.

Southwest Patrol Division covered approximately 13 square miles, bordered by the I-10 Freeway to the north, I-110 Freeway to the east, Vernon Avenue to the south, and La Cienega Boulevard to the west. This culturally diverse community had a population of approximately 165,000 residents who resided in the following neighborhoods and communities: Baldwin Village (formerly "The Jungle"), Baldwin Vista, Crenshaw Community, Jefferson Park, Leimert Park, Crenshaw District, West Adams Community and University Park (University of Southern California).

Southwest Area Reporting District Map

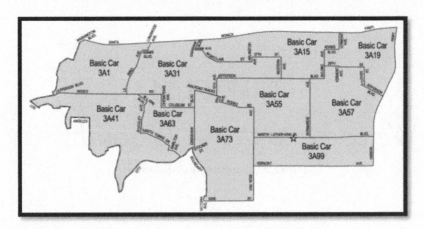

One of the ways to show initiative working patrol involved checking with the Divisional Detective's Unit to ascertain if there were any outstanding suspects they were looking for. I recalled making copies of wanted suspect's information disseminated during roll call out of the Rotator.

I focused in on a suspect wanted by Southwest Detectives for assault with a deadly weapon (ADW) Suspect on a Police Officer. According to the wanted bulletin, the suspect resided on Dalton Avenue, just south of Martin Luther King Boulevard, which was technically one block east of the station, I mean like walking distance!

Wanted Felon Captured

After roll call, I cleared the station to handle a couple of report calls. While on my way back to the station located at 1546 West Martin Luther King Boulevard, I drove eastbound through the alley south of Martin Luther King Boulevard toward Dalton Avenue.

As, I exited the mouth of alley and looked to my immediate right, low and behold I observed the wanted ADW suspect in his front yard raking leaves. You just can't make this sort of thing up. I continued to keep him under surveillance while simultaneously notifying Communications Division. I requested an air unit and two additional Southwest units to my location. Within minutes, the air unit had arrived overhead as well as numerous officers. The suspect was ordered into a felony prone position in his front yard at gunpoint. An arrest team moved in, and the suspect was taken into custody without incident. Just like that show me with one in custody!

I recalled the assigned detective asking me where did I locate the suspect. I told him the suspect was in his front yard raking leaves. It was always a good feeling to locate and arrest a wanted suspect without incident, especially a wanted, violent suspect! Soon, I would get introduced to The Jungle.

Welcome to The Jungle

Gangster Pep Talk: Check this out homeboys. I have good news and bad news for you. The good news first, I am permanently assigned to Southwest. The bad news is, I'm going to be here everyday and twice-on Sundays. I have no love for gangsters like you. Especially when you're strapped walking around like this is the Wild Wild West.

After completing my first deployment period, I was assigned to Unit 3A31, which patrolled several neighborhoods, including Baldwin Hills and The Jungle. These were two distinct neighborhoods. Baldwin Hills was an affluent neighborhood with multi-million dollar views. The Jungle consisted of a cluster of apartments occupied by the violent Bloods street gang and a Jamaican drug cartel. Through the years, the neighborhood reinvented itself, eventually becoming Baldwin Hills Village. The name change did not make it any safer. In any event, when I initially arrived at Southwest Patrol Division, an officer advised me "The Jungle" was too dangerous a neighborhood for officers to handle calls for service alone. The officer recommended I should avoid patrolling there without a partner.

Well, that sounded like a personal challenge to me. Our badge said, "Los Angeles Police Officer." I recall a robbery had just occurred in the 4800 block of August Street, which was right smack in the middle of The Jungle. I was assigned to Unit 3U1, a single officer report car. I informed Communications Division to show me en-route to the location. Upon my arrival, I told the assigned unit, whose suspect was gone, that I would interview the victim and complete the robbery preliminary investigation report. Both officers looked at me like I was crazy. I explained to them that I was big boy and not afraid to do my job. I carried a back-up weapon with plenty of ammunition.

I made it a point to qualify weekly at the Department's bonus firearm range. Training was a part of my daily regimen: run, lift weights, eat, sleep, and repeat. If you were going to work the streets of Los Angeles, the least you could do was stay in top physical condition, aka "Be patrol ready."

As I mentioned earlier, I was assigned to Unit 3A31. The car commander was my dear friend, Carlton Lawrence (RIP), a gentleman, outstanding father, partner, and human being. Carl was a great police officer as well. He was soft-spoken, easygoing and just an overall good partner.

The first day we worked together, I asked Carl to drive me around to all of the "asshole locations" within Southwest Patrol Division. Carl drove me around to all of the known hangouts of both Hispanic and Black street gangs. We finally drove into our assigned area of The Jungle. We stopped our patrol vehicle in front of 4828 August Street. I was seated in the passenger's seat. Our windows were rolled down when Carl called out to a Bloods gang member he recognized from numerous prior contacts.

As knucklehead began to walk up on my side of our patrol vehicle, he got the surprise of his life; I had already withdrawn my department firearm, a six-inch Smith & Wesson .38 caliber revolver. He was staring down my barrel, which was pointed at his upper torso. While I simultaneously exited the passenger's side of our vehicle, I ordered him to turn around, face away from me and not move. There was a second gangster with him who had dropped a firearm when we initially drove up and thought I did not notice that.

Carl told Communications Division, we were Code 6 on a 415 man with a gun. Both knuckleheads were detained at gunpoint and taken into custody without incident. I won't mention the actual Blood street gang, however, if you are familiar with The Jungle, you already know which gang hung out in that particular neighborhood. Making the above arrest gave me a chance to explain my gangster's philosophy to these knuckleheads and what they and others like them could expect from me on a daily basis.

Here is what I told them verbatim: "Check this out homeboys. I have good news and bad news for you. The good news first: I am permanently assigned to Southwest. The bad news is, I'm going to be here everyday and twice-on Sundays. I have no love for gangsters like you, especially when you're strapped walking around like this is the Wild Wild West."

The armed gangster taken into custody by Carl and I that day turned out to be an escaped felon. So, it was a good day when we captured numb nuts and took a firearm off the streets. I made it my business to learn all about that particular Bloods street gang.

Within months, I knew names, birthdates, monikers, and their associates. Back then, Bloods gang members from different areas hung out in The Jungle, which was known for the street sales of cocaine in rock form, marijuana and the occasional jewelry store smash and grab robberies.

There were a lot of violent crimes committed in and around the area. I was determined to do my part to negatively impact their criminal enterprise. There was a second criminal threat during that time too: numerous Jamaican cocaine dealers had moved into several apartments on a street called Gerber Place (not to be confused with Gerber's baby food).

Southwest patrol units would respond to shooting-in-progress calls from time to time that involved straight-up shootouts. Jamaican drug cartels and Bloods gang members were fighting to take control of the cocaine sales in the area. I recalled rolling to a shooting-in-progress on Gerber Place one late afternoon in

The Jungle. Upon our arrival, we could still smell fresh gunpowder in the air. An apartment had been shot up and abandoned in a hurry. We tactically deployed and entered the apartment to look for any shooting victims.

What we located were all sorts of illegal contraband, including a high-capacity magazine semi-automatic Uzi pistol, an AK-47 rifle, and pounds of marijuana. Fortunately, no one was shot on this particular day. The contraband was seized and booked into evidence.

Assault With A Deadly Weapon Suspect
(Violent ADW Suspect Arrested)

On September 22, 1986, I was working Unit 3A31. I made it a point to check with our divisional detectives daily to see if they had any outstanding wanted suspects that resided in or hung out in my basic car area. On the aforementioned date, I received information of a wanted suspect, who had brutally assaulted several victims in The Jungle area. The suspect was considered armed and dangerous.

Equipped with the information, my partner and I drove to The Jungle while it was still daylight to hunt for the suspect. While patrolling in the north-south alley between Gibraltar and Stevely Avenue, I observed the wanted suspect in a carport area. I immediately exited our police vehicle with my weapon drawn and pointed at the suspect, who had that "damn, damn, damn!" look on his face.

Communications Division was advised of our location and that we were in the process of taking an armed and dangerous suspect into custody. Initially, the suspect thought about running, but there was nowhere to go. I yelled out to him, "Sir, are you feeling OK? If you want to stay that way, you better get down your ass down on the ground right now with both hands where I can see them." The suspect was ordered into a felony prone position and was taken into custody without further incident. Subsequently, the victims contacted Southwest Station to thank us for arresting the suspect who had terrorized them.

By Deployment Period 10, I had obtained the best overall recap for the entire PM Watch. I loved my job and, back then; I probably would have worked for free. Simply stated, I enjoyed helping victims and witnesses who were unable to protect or defend themselves. My word was my bond. If a citizen told me something confidential, I would not disclose their identity at all costs. I would do my own due diligence to identify or establish probable cause to arrest suspects. Often, it would involve surveillance or just catching the knuckleheads red-handed with their illegal contraband, etc.

Death Threats Against The Police

As mentioned before, there were several other communities within Southwest Patrol Division that had their share of gang and narcotics activity. One specific Crips street gang had two different cliques. Their boundaries extended from Normandie Avenue to the east, Leimert Park to the west, Martin Luther King Boulevard to the north, and Vernon Avenue to the south. After attending a couple of Neighborhood Watch meetings and receiving information about gang and narcotics activity, we focused our attention on selective patrol enforcement, which meant a zero tolerance for illegal activity.

We made several gang-related observation arrests, seizing narcotics, money, and firearms. One special gangster, obviously upset with our proactive enforcement posture, lashed out by spray-painting my name on the Kentucky Fried Chicken restaurant on Leimert Park and Sutro Place. One thing was for certain: gangsters always liked to take credit for their artwork/graffiti. I felt honored to have my name written on the KFC along with "LAPD." Both had been crossed out. As a Los Angeles Police Officer, one of the most important skills you developed working the streets was reading graffiti. It is imperative as it can save your life and tell you what gangs were feuding. In this particular case, it allowed me to identify the gangster that authored the threat!

It was considered a badge of honor for a police officer to have a local gangster put their name on a wall or sidewalk. The average officer would have probably avoided the area altogether. However, I was not your average officer! Like, I mentioned earlier, the badge said "Police Officer–Los Angeles Police." I spent every available minute in the area of the threat conducting directed patrol. Well, my persistence paid off. One evening while driving through the east/west alley around 6th Avenue and south of Vernon Avenue, I located the graffiti artist, who had spray painted my name and "LAPD" on the KFC restaurant. Besides having a couple of outstanding warrants issued for his arrest, I took full advantage of our time together that evening. As you can imagine, he became emotional and started crying. I informed Mr. S for brains that threatening to kill a Los Angeles police officer could make him famous.

I taught knucklehead a valuable lesson that evening. I told him the quickest way to get a guaranteed reservation at 1104 N. Mission Road was to threaten the life of a Los Angeles police officer. He was inquisitive and wanted to know about 1104 North Mission Road. I guess he thought it was a new jail facility. He learned it was the Los Angeles County Coroner's Office. He ended up getting arrested during an unrelated caper and being sent to prison. Problem solved.

Crip Gang Member's Tribute to Me

Wife Alert

In August 1986, Officer Zevernik, aka "Z man," and I were working PM Watch patrol. Our shift started off good. We had driven into The Jungle and literally within 20 minutes had four gangsters in custody on different felony charges all in the backseat of our police vehicle. Like I said earlier, a full car was a happy car! In any event, I was driving on Santa Rosalia Drive at Marlton Avenue adjacent to the YMCA en route to the station when, I noticed this female exiting the front door of the YMCA. She had it going on. I turned to Z man and said, "Man those jeans look like there painted on! What do you think, Z man?" Some of the gangsters in our back seat stated, "She's proper Landrum." To which I replied, "I didn't recall asking for your opinions, so do me a favor and keep your pie hole shut!"

Knowing that I could not allow a beautiful woman to simply disappear into the evening without saying hello and hopefully getting her telephone number, I drove forward, parked at the curb, exited my patrol vehicle, and approached the passenger's side of her blue Mercury Zephyr. It should be noted that her mother was sitting in the passenger's side front seat. I introduced myself, greeted her mother, cleared my throat, and asked to speak to her alone.

When my soul mate exited the driver's door of her vehicle, I asked her for those seven magical digits. The rest is history. Thirty-three years later, we are still together married.

Kidnap~ Follow-Up~ Arrests

On the evening of August 14, 1987, I was assigned to Southwest Patrol Division working our Special Problems Unit (SPU). Sergeant Ted Spicer was our immediate supervisor. He briefed us during roll call that we might be working a human trafficking caper in the city of El Monte. It was contingent upon whether Detective Support Division's Special Investigation Section (SIS) would accept or decline to work it. According to the reporting party, they had paid a group of Coyotes to smuggle their 15-year-old loved one (a female) into the United States from Mexico. At some point, the Coyotes contacted the reporting party to demand additional money for the safe release of their loved one. The reporting party was given a particular timeframe to have the money or their loved one would be harmed.

SIS contacted the Southwest Patrol Division Watch Commander to advise that they would not be handling the Coyote caper. Sergeant Spicer was notified and called a Code Alpha. We responded to the station's parking lot and put together a tactical operations plan. The reporting party revealed she had been directed to drive into the parking lot of the Alpha Beta supermarket in El Monte to meet in-person with the suspects. There was just one little problem: the reporting party did not have any cash to pay the ransom request!

So, our SPU team was tasked with saving the day. Human trafficking/human smuggling was an inherently dangerous operation. We only had one chance; one shot, to get it right or the results could be deadly. We were on our way to conduct a follow-up in the city of El Monte after our supervisor contacted Detective Headquarters Division, Narcotics Information Network (NIN), and El Monte Police Department to advise all of those entities we would be conducting surveillance in the Alpha Beta supermarket parking lot on Dupree Avenue.

During our surveillance, the suspects drove up. The front passenger exited the suspect's vehicle and entered the rear passenger seat of the reporting person's vehicle. Eventually, the suspect exited the vehicle and reentered his vehicle. As they began to drive away, we got the OK to take the suspects down. We convened on the suspects, who decided to make a run for it. We had two black and white police vehicles standing by ready to pursue them as well as an LAPD air unit to support our operation. I was parked strategically in the eastern end of the parking lot in our dual-purpose police vehicle. We were deployed all around the Alpha Beta supermarket parking lot, ready to move in and arrest the suspects. Earlier, our designated point officer informed us that a vehicle had driven up next to our victim's vehicle. We got confirmation that the suspect had threatened to kill the reporting person's loved one.

After we got the green light to take down the suspects, we raced through the parking lot toward the suspect's vehicle with our forward-facing red light and siren on. We boxed in the suspect's vehicle, I exited my vehicle with my firearm pointing at the driver, and yelled, "Shut it down right now or get smoked right here, right now!" All bets were off when dealing with kidnap suspects and a victim's life hanging in the balance. There is no margin for error. We interrogated the suspects at the scene to obtain the location where the victim was being held. While en route, our supervisor requested additional units from the Los Angeles County Sheriff's Department.

Coyote's Wild

(Human Smuggling Coyote Caper)

Upon arriving to the location where we were told the victim was being held, we surrounded the place. A bullhorn was used to make contact with the occupants. Three additional suspects surrendered immediately and were taken into custody at gunpoint.

We entered the location in order to locate the 15-year-old kidnap victim. To our surprise, we located the victim along with approximately 16 other individuals, who were locked in three different bedrooms within the residence, all being held against their will. U. S. Customs and Border Protection was contacted, responded, and took custody of the 17 immigrants, who had been smuggled into the United States illegally. Our five suspects were arrested for various felony criminal charges, including kidnapping and were turned over to the U.S. Customs and Border Protection. Mission accomplished!

Promotion

On Sunday, December 6, 1987, approximately one year, four months and eleven days after being transferred into Southwest Patrol Division, I was promoted to the rank of Police Officer III. During that time, LAPD was going through budgetary issues and there was a shortage of training officers. Captain Nick Salikois contacted me via telephone to give me the good news.

There were five temporary training officer positions and one permanent position. I was promoted to the permanent position effective immediately. I showed up for roll call and everyone looked at me with my brand new PIII stripes on my uniform shirtsleeves and jacket. I laughed and said, "Don't hate the player fellas, just the game! I got the permanent position. Nothing temporary about that, my brothers!"

Robbery/GTA Just Occurred

On the morning of Friday, January 29, 1988, I was working Southwest morning watch patrol, assigned to Unit 3A31 with my partner Police Officer III Paul Lawson (RIP). I think of Robocop, when I think of Lawson; he was the ultimate police professional. Paul was a dedicated husband, father, grandfather, brother, partner and FTO. He was the senior officer on our car as well as a distinguished firearm expert. Immediately following roll call, Communications Division put out this crime broadcast:

"Any Southwest unit available to handle, a 211/ GTA just occurred from the Shell gas station located at Normandie Avenue and King Boulevard. Suspects are described as one male and two female Blacks armed with a blue steel large-caliber revolver. Vehicle taken is described as a 1988, four-door, gray, Ford Escort, with a Schaffer Ford

license plate frame, no plates. Last seen north-bound on Normandie Avenue."

Lawson and I cleared the station. It was my night to drive, so we headed out to the Arco station, located on the Southeast corner of Crenshaw Boulevard and Jefferson Boulevard to grabbed a couple of sandwiches; some Gatorade and vitamin packs before showing ourselves clear to handle radio calls.

211/GTA Vehicle Following and Arrests

There is an old saying in police work that timing is everything! As I exited the Arco station parking lot onto northbound Crenshaw Boulevard and drove into the northbound left-hand turn lane, there was one other vehicle in front of our patrol vehicle. At first glance, I thought I was dreaming. Right there in front of us was the 211/GTA vehicle with two of the three suspects inside. What a gift! I alerted Lawson, who notified Communications Division that we were now following the 211/GTA vehicle westbound on Jefferson Boulevard from Crenshaw Boulevard. Lawson broadcasted our unit's destination and location and a description of the suspect's vehicle.

After Communications Division acknowledged Lawson, he requested an air unit and additional units as the suspect's vehicle continued driving westbound on Jefferson Boulevard past Victoria Avenue before suddenly turning left onto Somerset Drive southbound towards 36th Street. As the suspect's vehicle approached 36th Street, we observed the driver toss a large-caliber revolver out of the driver's side window while turning right onto 36th Street.

Lawson updated Communications Division of our location and requested a unit respond to Somerset Drive at 36th Street to recover the suspect's discarded firearm. Moments later, the suspect pulled over to the north curb on 36th Street between Somerset Drive and Wellington Road. Responding units were advised to respond westbound only from Somerset Drive at 36th Street to avoid cross-fire. Usually when a suspect decides to stop suddenly, you have to be physically and mentally prepared for the real possibility of an officer-involved shooting, foot pursuit, or use of force.

Since these were armed robbery suspects, I deployed the department shotgun, chambered a round into the barrel, released the safety, and took up a position of advantage behind the driver's door of our police vehicle. Lawson had deployed his service revolver and had taken a position of advantage behind the passenger's door of our police vehicle.

As additional units arrived, Lawson began to give the suspects verbal commands and ordered them out of the vehicle, one at a time. The suspects were taken into custody without incident and the discarded revolver recovered. Detectives were able to follow up and identify the third, outstanding suspect. The victim's vehicle was recovered and returned to him. I worked with Lawson for a couple more deployment periods before returning to PM watch. I was reassigned into the SPU, this time as an FTO.

Shots Fired into an Occupied Dwelling Suspect

Tuesday (Suspect Arrested)

On March 15, 1988, my partner Police Officer I Deborah McGuire and I were assigned to Southwest Patrol Division. We monitored a crime broadcast involving shots fired into an inhabited dwelling, which occurred in Wilshire Patrol Division. The crime broadcast identified the suspect as Carl Hightower. According to the crime broadcast, Hightower was driving a possible early '70's model Chevrolet, headed to a home at 2630 South Dalton Avenue, located in the northern section of Southwest Patrol Division.

McGuire and I responded to the area to conduct surveillance at the above-mentioned location. While doing so, I observed a white Ford Mustang drive up and park in front of the home. A single male Black adult exited the vehicle. Although the crime broadcast disclosed that the vehicle was an early '70's model Chevrolet, I decided to conduct an investigative stop on the individual to eliminate him as a suspect. I directed McGuire, who notified Communications Division that we were Code 6 on the possible suspect from the shots-fired-into-an-inhabited-dwelling incident from Wilshire Patrol Division. It was quickly determined the individual now detained was, in fact, Carl Hightower.

While being taken into custody, Hightower made several spontaneous and incriminating statements that placed him at the scene of the shooting. During the inventory search of his vehicle, I located and recovered a loaded shotgun. Hightower was booked and charged for California Penal Code § 246, a felony shooting into an inhabited dwelling, booking number 9546199.

CHAPTER 15

39th Street and Dalton Avenue

(Newsworthy Search Warrant)

This incident, which occurred on Monday, August 1, 1988, involved serving several gang-related search warrants in direct response to a gang related shooting, during which an innocent victim's home with his family present inside was shot up. After the shooting, an investigation was launched, resulting in the procurement of a multiple-locations search warrant. During the search pre-planning, the Area Commanding Officer requested a mandatory meeting, where we were informed to make the search warrant locations uninhabitable. Now, imagine the same Area Commanding Officer tells you and your fellow officers that if you somehow become involved in an officer-involved shooting during the search warrant service, it would not be scrutinized or investigated like other officer-involved-shootings. Would you feel comfortable?

Well, standby to standby: You are about to read about one of the most infamous search warrants ever served by members of the Los Angeles Police Department. Here is the true story behind 39th Street and Dalton Avenue. There have been numerous news articles written by the *Los Angeles Times* that publically identified the Southwest Area Commanding Officer involved as, Captain III Thomas Elfmont. The city of Los Angeles would pay out approximately four million dollars in damages as a direct result of this particular search warrant service.

Reason Behind 39th Street and Dalton Avenue

Here's how it all began: The area of 39th Street and Dalton Avenue was a known hangout for one of the many violent Crips street gangs in Southwest Patrol Division. Besides their involvement in shooting, assaults, robberies, and murders, they were major players in the street sales of cocaine and marijuana. Between the months of June and July 1988, a Hispanic family had purchased a home at 3905 Dalton Avenue in Los Angeles. The new occupants' residence was between two apartment buildings, 3903-3903 ½ Dalton Avenue to the north and 3907-3907 ½ Dalton Avenue to the south. The apartments were known hangouts for gang members from a violent local Crips street gang.

Victim Threatened by Local Gangsters

Meanwhile, the victim was a proud new homeowner and decided to trim the palm trees in front of his residence for better curb appeal. While doing so, he was approached by several members of the Crips, who told him to stop trimming his palm trees, because they used them to conceal their illegal narcotics from the police. The victim felt intimidated and immediately stopped. The next day, he decided to install security lights around his home as a crime deterrent.

Shots Fired Into An Inhabited Dwelling

After the victim-installed security lighting, the gangsters approached him again. This time, they warned him about the lights, which could illuminate them when officers were patrolling the area at night. The victim ignored their demands, which unfortunately resulted in his residence being shot up (What a cowardly and senseless act of violence!). The night of the shooting, Southwest Patrol Officers responded and completed their preliminary investigation. A crime report was taken, and Detective Carl Sims and his partner, Detective Bob Clark, were assigned to conduct the follow-up investigation.

Probationary Officers Go Undercover

During that time, I was assigned to SPU and had a new probationary officer, Dennis Aleman. Both Aleman and another new probationary officer, Robert Hernandez, spoke fluent Spanish. Detective Sims learned through his follow-up investigation that the Crip gang members were responsible for the shooting and were involved in selling marijuana and cocaine out of the apartments. Detective Sims began work to procure a search warrant, and, since Aleman and Hernandez spoke fluent Spanish, it was decided they should go undercover as the victim's family members to gather probable cause for the search warrants. They would essentially become the search warrant affiants (persons who swear to an affidavit) for the multi-location search warrants. Their primary mission was to document and identify the suspects, their pattern of conduct and the locations involved to assist Detective Sims with collecting the factual evidence he needed to procure the multi-location search warrants. The ultimate goal was to shut down the illegal activity, arrest those responsible for the shooting, and restore normalcy and safety back to the entire community.

In the meantime, we were providing extra patrol in the area to protect our undercover officers and the victim's family. Thanks to Aleman and Hernandez, Detective Sims gathered the information needed. Based on the illegal gang and narcotics activity, Detective Sims decided the search warrants would be served on August 1, 1988, when the suspects would most likely be heavily involved in the street sales of their cocaine and marijuana.

Operation Hammer-Gang Taskforce

Looking back at that era of policing, violent street gang-related crimes and homicides were increasing. In an effort to reduce the fear and incidents of crime, South Bureau's Deputy Chief William Rathburn created the taskforce Operation Hammer. Basically, the Operation Hammer-Gang Taskforce consisted of numerous police officers and supervisors loaned from South Bureau, who saturated high-crime and gang areas within Southwest, 77th Street, Southeast, and Harbor Patrol divisions. There were approximately 70 to 80 officers assigned to this taskforce. There was a zero-tolerance enforcement policy for gangs and other illegal activities.

The strategy had been effective to a certain degree and temporarily reduced crime rates in certain areas. Detective Sims began to put together his search warrant operational plan with his partner, Detective Clark. Due to the multiple locations, he needed additional resources and made the request to his superiors. There had been street rumors that a specific, heavily armed Crips street gang had threatened to kill a Los Angeles Police Officer.

The Infamous Captain's Meeting

WARNING BELLS: "If an officer-involved shooting occurs, the Bureau would not scrutinize or look at it as closely as other shootings due to the gang involvement."

One afternoon in July 1988, Sergeant Spicer notified members of our SPU team that Captain Elfmont had called a mandatory meeting. The captain wanted to privately meet with us to discuss the pending search warrant service scheduled for Monday, August 1.

Keep in mind that our SPU team had served dozens and dozens of search warrants at numerous gangster locations, so we were all wondering what made this particular search warrant service so special. At that time, I had approximately five years on the job and many of the other officers assigned to our SPU team had less time than me. However, they were all squared away; I would take a door with any one of them, any day of the week. We all sat silently, as Captain Elfmont spoke to us about his expectations for the upcoming search warrant service. Back in 1988, if you told Los Angeles Police Officers to dig a ditch, it would get done!

Make Those Locations Uninhabitable!

Captain Elfmont began to address our SPU team. We were sitting there with our eyes wide open as he began saying that this particular Crips street gang needed to be taught a lesson. Captain Elfmont stated, "I want you to make those locations uninhabitable. Whatever happens, upper management would not hold it against you!" As he continued talking, I thought to myself, "This has got to be a joke. He can't be serious." I was not aware of any captain, lieutenant, or sergeant for that matter that felt comfortable enough to make such a bold statement to a bunch of young, impressionable police officers. As I looked around the room, I noticed that everyone else present had the exact same look on their faces as I did—shock. This was a captain of police addressing a group of young police officers about destroying property during a search warrant. As mentioned earlier, in my mind, I kept thinking, Captain Elmont has to be kidding. But he wasn't! In fact, I believe he meant every single word spoken during our meeting.

Proceed with Caution

As we continued to listen, Captain Elfmont made another troubling falsehood when he stated, "If an officer-involved shooting occurs, the Bureau would not look at it as closely as other shootings, due to the gang involvement." At that point, I thought to myself, what a profound statement! The Los Angeles Police Department's Officer-involved Shooting Policy was crystal clear and straight-forward. Nothing had changed from the time I had attended and graduated from the Los Angeles Police Academy. The department's shooting policy was predicated on two acronyms, B.A.L.K.S. and IDOL, as well as, the California Penal Code. These acronyms are still applied today:

Background	**I**mmediate **D**efense **O**f **L**ife
Age of suspect	
Last Resort	
Knowledge of Crime	
Seriousness of Crime	

Anything outside of the department's policy and the law could definitely result in criminal and administrative investigations. For example, if an officer was involved in a shooting and stated, "<u>Uh, the reason, I shot the suspect was because our captain told me the bureau would not scrutinize or look at it as closely as other shootings due to the gang involvement</u>," do you think for a hot minute, that statement would justify the shooting? I could guarantee you; the officer would be terminated from employment and most likely would be criminally charged and sued for their irresponsible actions. The captain on the other hand would probably deny they made such a statement!

SPU Team Meeting (Southwest Parking Lot)

"Don't go beyond the scope and nature of the search warrant. Forget about making the place uninhabitable. That's not our job."

After listening to Captain Elfmont's misguided search warrant pep talk, some of us met in the parking lot to debrief what we had just heard. I personally thought his statements were controversial. I told everyone, "Don't go beyond the scope and nature of the search warrant. Forget about making the place uninhabitable. That's not our job." Remember your Academy firearm training, we are all held personally responsible for every single round fired out of our duty weapons." I reaffirmed that no one, including a Captain of Police, could tell you when to shoot a weapon. That was a personal decision.

With regards to the search warrant service itself, I told our team to just follow department policy, rules, and procedures. Sergeant Spicer was one of the best supervisors that I had ever worked for. He was squared away and always followed department policy. He understood the meaning of ethics and integrity. It was because of him, that I wanted to become a sergeant.

Search Warrant Service Time

(39th Street and Dalton Avenue)

The day of the search warrants, we are all poised and ready to serve them. Detective Sims was able to get what was known as nighttime endorsement, which meant that due to articulable facts, we were able to serve the search warrants during the hours of darkness. Most search warrants are served between the hours of 0700 hours to 2200 hours, unless there exists an exigent circumstance involving a danger to the community or law enforcement officers. Having nighttime endorsement technically meant we could serve the search warrants at 0200 hours in the morning if that was the best time for us.

To cut down on numerous police vehicles in the area and to prevent an ingress and egress tactical situation, we had procured an old DWP work van and outfitted it with a bench to transport arrestees, as well as a storage area to keep our search warrant entry tools, like large bolt cutters, crowbars, cord cuffs, and the Key to the City aka "The Ram."

Los Angeles Times' Misconception

During a review of the majority of news articles written about the 39th Street and Dalton Avenue incident, I found that articles often identified the Southwest SPU team as the only group of officers that executed the search warrants and were solely responsible for the destruction of property at the locations. Well, I'm here to clarify and correct the record. Earlier, I mentioned that Detective Carl Sims had requested the assistance of personnel from the Operation Hammer-Gang Taskforce with the service of the search warrants due to multiple locations.

Please note that the Southwest SPU team included me and six other officers. Some of the officers on SPU had been assigned to perimeter containment, and the rest were assigned to the entry team at 3903 South Dalton Avenue. The Operation Hammer-Gang Taskforce, on the other hand, were responsible for entering and searching the other three locations identified as, 3903½, 3907 and 3907½ Dalton Avenue.

Trojan Horse

(House Call Time)

KNOCK AND NOTICE: "This is the Los Angeles Police Department, we have a search warrant for 3903 Dalton Avenue. Open the door. LAPD search warrant! We are demanding entry. Open the door now!"

We were staged in the parking lot at Southwest Patrol Division awaiting the green light to respond to our search warrant location to take care of business. Finally, at approximately 2030 hours or 8:30 p.m., we loaded up and drove our converted utility police response van to the location. Since this was a dynamic search warrant entry, we ran into position with the entry team, ready to make entry.

I knocked on the front door of 3903 South Dalton Avenue, our assigned location and announced our presence. "This is the Los Angeles Police Department. We have a search warrant for 3903 Dalton Avenue. Open the door! LAPD, search warrant. We are demanding entry! Open the door now!"

I waited a reasonable time and, due to the circumstances and my personal experience that suspects often ignore your verbal commands to buy time to flush their contraband down the toilet, I made a command decision and used our ram to forcibly open the front door. I recalled the door busting open from the force of being struck on the doorknob. As a result of the force, the door struck the interior wall, causing one of the door's windowpanes to shatter.

In the meantime, SPU officers initiated their dynamic entry and announced their presence while ascending the interior apartment stairs. The plan called for myself and a couple of other officers to stand by outside to help guard the detained suspects at the search warrant locations. Within a few minutes, we discovered that our primary suspect was not located within the residence, which belonged to his sister, Gloria Flowers. But she was there—in the bathroom. The scene was somewhat chaotic because gang task force officers were all over the place. As things began to settle down, the entire street was locked down, and a large crowd of onlookers had gathered. I surveyed the crowd and observed Hildebrandt Flowers being taken into custody by an officer on the perimeter. That gang task force officer and I escorted Hildebrandt to the front yard of 3903 South Dalton Avenue.

Major Lack of Communication

The search warrant had too many moving parts. I never spoke with Detective Sims on the night of the search warrant about where Hildebrandt had been located and arrested. I recalled Officer Lemmer notifying Sergeant Spicer during the search about damage to the bathroom toilet in 3903 South Dalton Avenue; he had inadvertently damaged the toilet while searching for contraband. I informed Sergeant Spicer about the shattered windowpanes and damaged front door, which occurred during entry. It was customary during any search warrant conducted by our Southwest SPU Team to have Sergeant Spicer conduct a walk through to check the location for any damages or anything that could be considered a city/civil liability and to document that damage.

There were several suspects that had been taken into custody and loaded into our van to be transported to Southwest Station. I had been reassigned to complete a different mission. During the course of the search warrant, my probationer, Aleman was still working in an undercover capacity inside the victim's residence.

Sergeant Spicer had directed me and two other officers to go back to the station to change into plain clothes with LAPD raid jackets and re-deploy down the street to keep an eye on the victim's residence in the event of a payback/retaliation incident.

Andy Griffith Tunes

As mentioned earlier, all suspects detained were loaded up in our SPU van and transported to Southwest Station to be booked. I rode back in the van with the suspects. Upon our arrival, we ordered them out into a single-file line. The suspects were ordered to whistle the *Andy Griffith* tune as they were being escorted into the station.

I thought it was hilarious, gangsters whistling the *Andy Griffith* tune. However, the Department failed to find the humor in that. Personally, it made my entire night. Laughter was good for the soul! Well, back to reality. I still had one important mission left to complete. That mission was to ensure the safety of the undercover officers Aleman and Hernandez.

Search Warrant Location Property Vandalized

It was now close to midnight. Officer Todd Clease, myself and another police officer sat inside a blue Ford Taurus monitoring the search warrant location, which had been cleared by all law enforcement personnel. There were several people gathered in the front yard at 3903 and 3903½ South Dalton Avenue. An unidentified male began ripping open a couch that was in the front yard. I kept thinking to myself, why would there be a couch in the front yard, and why was that guy ripping it open? I notified Sergeant Spicer of my observations via my handheld Rover radio over Simplex, which was a person-to-person frequency, not recorded.

Sergeant Spicer advised us to just monitor the situation. Our primary mission was to ensure the safety of Aleman and Hernandez. Around 1 a.m., we cleared the location safely and went end of watch along with Aleman and Hernandez.

Television News Conference

The Aftermath

"Obviously there was misconduct that occurred here! The Department will be conducting a full and thorough internal investigation, and those

responsible will be held accountable!" ~Deputy Chief William Rathburn

I woke up the next morning and began making breakfast. I turned on my television set and started channel surfing, looking for something to watch, when all of a sudden, Channel 2 News was conducting a live press conference in the front yards of 3907 and 3907½ South Dalton Avenue, Los Angeles. Initially, I thought this couldn't be real as I stared at the television. I thought to myself, "This can't be real: A news conference taking place in the front yards of last night's multiple search warrant locations."

There was even a City of Los Angeles podium set up in the front yard. As the cameras began to capture the new conference, I observed Deputy Chief Rathburn standing at the podium in full uniform flanked in the background by Captain Elfmont and, I believe, Commander Matthew Hunt. Channel 2 News began to show live footage of the aftermath of the search warrants, which was truly disturbing. Some of the locations did appear to be uninhabitable.

POP QUIZ

Question: Now, why would officers go beyond the scope and nature of a search warrant to intentionally destroy property?

Answer: If your answer was "Because of the Captain's direct orders at the pre-search warrant meeting," you're probably correct! Officers had taken his words as a direct order to make the places uninhabitable. There was no misinterpreting or misunderstanding of what was said in plain English!

Like I mentioned earlier, during that era of policing, if you gave Los Angeles Police Officers specific or general directions to do something—in this case, make a place uninhabitable under the false pretense that the Department would back you 100%—unfortunately, some officers would follow that order. It was obvious several of the Operation Hammer-Gang Taskforce officers took the captain's words to heart.

LA Times Articles: Southwest Captain Thomas Elfmont, just five months on the job, encouraged his officers to take back the block. Some of his officers recall Elfmont telling them before the raid to render the buildings "uninhabitable." He denies ever saying that!

Question: How many of you believe the captain stepped up after the news conference and told his immediate supervisors, Deputy Chief Rathburn and Commander Matthew Hunt about his pre-search warrant meetings with officers under his direct span of control?

Answer: It never occurred until we were all interviewed by Internal Affairs Group! According to *Los Angeles Times* reporter Mitchell (March 2001), "Elfmont now says that was a mistake. The problem was, no one was in charge to execute the search warrant, he said. There should have been at least a lieutenant on hand."

The article also states, "Southwest Captain Thomas Elfmont, just five months on the job, encouraged his officers to take back the block. Some of his officers recall Elfmont telling them before the raid to render the buildings 'uninhabitable.' He denies ever saying that."

Meanwhile, Deputy Chief Rathburn was visibly upset when he made the below statement during the news conference, "Obviously there was misconduct that occurred here! The Department will be conducting a full and thorough internal investigation and those responsible will be held accountable!" Our worst fear had come true. The execution of the search warrants had gone south and everyone was about to be held accountable for his or her actions.

Special Investigation
(Internal Investigation No. 88-1485)

On Tuesday, August 2, 1988, the day after the search warrant service. I drove into the parking lot at Southwest Police Station, grabbed my clean uniform, and began to walk toward the rear door of the station. Upon reaching the rear door, I was greeted by a sergeant of police, who directed me to respond immediately to Operations-South Bureau (OSB) to be interviewed. Back then; OSB was the headquarters for Southwest, 77th Street, Southeast, Harbor, and South Traffic divisions. Assigned to each bureau of command were a Deputy Chief and a Commander. Together, they were responsible for the overall day-to-day operations within South Bureau. OSB was located across from the University of Southern California in a shopping center north of Jefferson Boulevard at McClintock Avenue.

At this point, I was a little concerned about being interviewed. Obviously, I knew it had something to do with the August 1st search warrants. Upon entering the offices at OSB, I observed several other officers waiting. There were a lot of suits walking around with yellow, letter-sized legal notepads. An older gentleman, who identified himself as Sergeant Bob Kavanagh from the Employee Representative Section, greeted us.

According to Kavanagh, he was there to represent us while we were being interviewed. For the majority of us, this was the first time we had been in any serious trouble. Kavanagh told us not to worry. I headed into an office to be interviewed. I recall being interviewed by two investigators assigned to Internal Affairs Division.

At that point, I was told the interview was a "special investigation." I would soon learn that a special investigation was still an Internal Affairs Personnel Complaint involving then unidentified officers. As the investigation advanced, officers were named and accused of misconduct. During the initial interview, we were asked about our duty and assignment on Monday, August 1, 1988. Basically, we told investigators a step-by-step of who, what, where, when, why, and how.

Handwriting Exemplars Requested

At some point during my interview, one of the IA investigators provided me with a clean sheet of white paper and a black marker. I was ordered to write the words, "San Dog" and "LAPD Rules" on the blank piece of paper.

In my mind I'm like, "What the hell is really going on?" Next, I was shown photographs of shear destruction inside of the apartments searched on South Dalton Avenue. The investigators wanted to know if I had anything to do with either of the residences during the search warrant or did I have any first-hand knowledge about what happened. I explained that I never entered any of the locations during the search warrant. Furthermore, I advised them that members of the Southwest SPU Team only entered 3903 South Dalton Avenue and that a toilet had been damaged, as well as, the front door during the initial entry, which was reported to our immediate supervisor, Sergeant Spicer. I advised them that members from the Operation Hammer-Gang Taskforce were responsible for the search warrant services at the other three locations on Dalton Avenue.

They showed me additional photographs of drywall with large holes and at least one television set with a busted picture tube with red paint transfer on it. Imagine living in one of the upstairs units, opening your rear door only to see your porch/landing and stairs were no longer attached to the building. I agreed that was some bullshit right there! I didn't sign up to purposely destroy folks' property.

That's exactly what occurred at the 3907 and 3907½ South Dalton Avenue locations. The outdoor wooden porch/landing and stairs had been torn down during the search warrant service. There was absolutely no legitimate reason for such destruction. Those actions were completely unacceptable.

Personally, I was shocked at the level of destruction that had taken place. I remember saying that this is not what LAPD was all about. As a members of the Southwest Special Problems Unit, we had served numerous gang-related search warrants without incident or destruction.

A couple of months prior to the 39th Street and Dalton Avenue search warrants being served, our entire SPU team had received several commendations, including one written by Deputy Chief William Rathburn.

06/30/1988	COMMENDATION
Southwest SPU Units obviously well trained and supervised. Officers commended for outstanding field tactics, safety skills, and teamwork in arrest of narcotics traffickers.	
07/13/1988	COMMENDATION
Chief Rathburn note w/ commendation for SPU accomplishments with "Anytime and Place" Motto. Gang Task Force reduced crime and danger in community.	

Judgment Day

Adjudication (IA No. 88-1485)

Oh well, there is an old police metaphor, "One Ah Shit, wipes out a dozen Atta Boys!" It was apparent: Deputy Chief William Rathburn wanted his pound of flesh, and rightfully so. There were a lot of officers accused of misconduct including me. A couple of the officers *not* assigned to Southwest SPU, were terminated for their actions during the infamous 39th Street and Dalton Avenue search warrant debacle.

REAL TALK: "A lot of the adjudicators reviewing our complaint investigation hadn't been out in the field in years—except to go to lunch—let alone served a high-risk gangster search warrant."

I was accused of two counts of Unbecoming Conduct of an Officer after admitting to being apart of the *Andy Griffith* tune serenade and for allegedly not waiting a reasonable time before making forcible entry into our search warrant location. Although it was a dynamic entry, the powers that be felt I should have waited longer. Anyone, who has served search warrants on a regular basis, knows it's a judgment call by the entry team leader.

Real Talk: A lot of the adjudicators reviewing our complaint investigation hadn't been out in the field in years— except to go to lunch—let alone served a high-risk gangster search warrant. Several officers faced discipline.

I recalled Kavanagh telling all of us that Chief Daryl F. Gates himself extended the offer of 10 suspension days as opposed to being sent to a Board of Rights (BOR), aka Kangaroo Court. I'm not a gambler, so I decided it would be in my best interest and smart to just take my medicine.

On Tuesday, October 11, 1988, approximately two months and ten days after the infamous search warrants, I signed for the (10) days' suspension and moved on with my life. However, looking back now, I should have requested a BOR hearing just like some of the other officers, who were found not guilty on all counts alleged against them. The investigation disclosed that a small group of officers caused 90% of the damage that evening. The city of Los Angeles ended up paying out a little over 4.4 million dollars in punitive damages to a bunch of gangsters and other innocent folks—LAPD Lotto!

Criminal Charges

Sadly, criminal charges were filed against our supervisor, as well as a police officer that had been assigned to Operation Hammer-Gang Taskforce and Area Commanding Officer Captain Elfmont. I was subpoenaed as a witness, along with numerous officers and recall being interviewed by Department Adjutant Sonny Cookson, who allowed us to review our statement given to investigators during our original interviews as well as the arrest report from that night. That was the first time that I saw or read the actual arrest report. Up to that point, I had never seen the actual arrest report written by Detective Carl Sims. One thing that I pointed out that was incorrect was on the night of August 1st; Hildebrandt Flowers was found loitering on the street among the crowd and was detained by me and another officer. Hildebrandt had been escorted to the front yard of 3903 and 3903½ South Dalton Avenue where the other gangsters were detained. There was a total lack of communication on that particular night. I never made it known or clear to Detective Sims that Hildebrandt was not located inside of his sister's apartment. That would explain why Sims had assumed he was located there. We all loved and respected our sergeant then and now! We told the truth, and many of the involved officers wished the trials had been bifurcated so Captain Elfmont would be tried alone, just like he abandoned us. We were all thankful that our sergeant was acquitted on all charges filed against him. Captain Elfmont was acquitted as well.

39th Street and Dalton Avenue Final Assessment

On the evening of August 1, 1988, the Span of Control was impossible for one, two, or even three supervisors to manage effectively. Where were the other sergeants and lieutenants from our neighboring patrol divisions? The Operation Hammer-Gang Taskforce was made up of numerous officers, who were on loan from other South Bureau Patrol Divisions. It probably would have been a good idea to deploy their supervisors. Let's not forget about Captain Elfmont. Remember, he was the current Area Commanding Officer for Southwest Patrol Division. I remember someone mentioning Captain Elfmont disclosed that he had forgotten all about the search warrant and had made an appointment with his interior decorator for his home. Really! His subordinates were all involved in a major search warrant service, and he was no place to be found.

However, he was available the following day of the infamous search warrants for interviews with local news channels to discuss officer misconduct! Well, imagine that! What ever happened to attention to duty, leading by example, and more importantly, personal ethics, integrity and accountability?

ARISTOTLE: "Ethics is doing the right thing, in the right manner, for the right reasons, under the right circumstances."

As officers, we were held to a higher standard and now were being held accountable for our actions. Captain Elfmont had a different standard. Apparently, his entire defense was that officers misunderstood or misinterpreted what he had said. If you believe that, then I would like to sell you some property in Chernobyl next to the Nuclear Power Plant for pennies on the dollar. We were all educated and understood exactly what he meant and more importantly what he said. He let us all down and turned his back on all of us, especially when we needed help!

Picking Up The Pieces

The 39th Street and Dalton Avenue incident will be viewed as one of the worst search warrant services ever conducted by members of the Los Angeles Police Department. However, it was time to pick up the pieces and move forward. I was still in the business of protecting and serving the citizens of Los Angeles. Violent crimes, homicides, robberies, and narcotics trafficking did not cease after the search warrant service. In fact, there was an increase in all Part-I crimes. I returned from my 10-days suspension a little poorer, but still motivated and interested in doing the right thing!

During my tenure as a Field Training Officer, I had the opportunity to train some of the finest police officers in the world. Four of my former probationers were selected for the Elite Metropolitan Division's Special Weapons and Tactics Team: Michael Baker, Joel Martinez, Wilson Wong, and Keith Provin. It's a badge of honor knowing that I had the opportunity to train those go-getters while assigned to Southwest Patrol Division. Now, it was time for me to learn a new trick.

Loan to Detectives

Captain Elmont was demoted from Captain III to Captain II, administratively transferred to Valley Traffic Division, which ended his career ascent. He would eventually retire as the Commanding Officer of Communications Division. Southwest would get an entirely new command staff, Area Commanding Officer Captain III Noel Cunningham and Patrol Commanding Officer Captain I J.I. Davis. During the Southwest's annual Christmas Party, I thought, it's time to do something different. So, I introduced myself to Captain Cunningham and requested a meeting with him to talk about my future on the job. Within the week, I met with Captain Cunningham and laid all my cards on the table. I wanted a chance to work with detectives, and Captain Cunningham gave me that fresh start.

That next deployment period, I was on loan to Southwest detectives assigned to the robbery detail. Detective III Jerry Anslow was the Robbery Section Coordinator; my assigned Detective Training Officer was Detective II Kenny Hamilton, an outstanding detective with many years of investigative experience. I was eager to learn and took the initiative to read the LAPD Detective Manual from cover to cover.

Being assigned to work detectives was a great career change for me. Crime reports were divided into two categories: Category One (involving an arrestee) and Category Two (investigated only when all Category One cases had been handled). We were not required to routinely contact Category Two victims. Since, my expertise was gangs, I handled the majority of crimes involving gang members. Southwest Patrol Division, like all South-end divisions, experienced an uptick in gang-related drive-by shootings. Our Detective Commanding Officer, Lieutenant II Alan B. Kerstein, decided to do something about it. Lieutenant Kerstein procured additional resources, and the Southwest Drive-by Shooting Team was launched.

CHAPTER 16

Drive-by Shooting Team

I was soon assigned to PM Watch Detectives. Our immediate supervisor was Detective II Campbell. Police Officers Donald Williams, David Rosenberg, Guillermo (Memo) Galvan, and Raymond Marquez were loaned from Patrol to Detectives as apart of the newly launched Drive-by Shooting Team. Lieutenant Kerstein had assembled a group of officers with gang expertise to cover all of the street gangs within Southwest Patrol's jurisdiction. We had Bloods and Crips street gangs feuding, Hispanic street gangs feuding against one another, as well as, Black versus Brown gang violence. Basically, as the gangsters say, "It was on and popping!"

We learned quickly that today's victims were tomorrow's suspects! The majority of the time, when investigating gang-related shootings, it was like pulling sensitive teeth. Gangsters would always claim they did not know who shot them or their homeboys. We would drive around the neighborhood, check out the graffiti and review other crime reports. We solved a lot of gang-related shootings.

Halloween Night
(Fatal Officer-involved Shooting)

On Wednesday, October 31, 1990, I requested the evening off to take my little angel trick or treating. In the meantime, gang violence was still running rampant in Southwest Patrol Division between the Bloods vs. Crips, Hispanics vs. Hispanics, and Blacks vs. Hispanics. There were several street beefs happening within Southwest Patrol Division. My partners Donald Williams and David Rosenberg decided to work on that particular Halloween night. Ray had taken the night off and Lieutenant Kerstein directed Memo to take off due to his maximum overtime accumulation.

Our unit was all about reducing the fear and incidents of crime. To that end, often we would rent vehicles from a local car rental company named Ugly Duckling Rent-A-Car, which suited the vehicles in their fleet precisely. You wouldn't want anyone you knew to see you driving around in these beauties. Some had dents, others had paint transfer from God only knows what, and the upholstery in most was in bad repair.

However, their vehicles were perfect for our mission of rolling around in the neighborhood to fit in as we conducted surveillance. It was no secret that gang violence had become a major focal point throughout South Bureau. The Los Angeles Police Department was committed to doing its part to reduce gang violence, which had begun to impact the lives of people who lived, worked, and visited our many diverse communities. So, Williams and Rosenberg were in plain clothes working undercover doing what we did on a normal evening. They were conducting a follow-up investigation on one of their assigned gang-related cases. It was about 8:00 p.m., night had fallen upon the city, and parents were out with their costumed children going door-to-door trick or treating.

Meanwhile, Williams was driving and Rosenberg was the passenger officer in their Ugly Duckling Rent-A-Car. While traveling in the area of Adams Boulevard near Hoover Avenue, they observed two male Hispanic gang members walking in the crosswalk mad dogging and throwing up flashing gang signals with their hands at a group of male Hispanics in a vehicle at the traffic light. As the officers continued to monitor what was unfolding, one of the male Hispanics in a gray Chevrolet vehicle exited the vehicle with both of his hands wrapped in a towel and extended outward.

Based on his actions, Williams and Rosenberg truly believed the suspect was armed and about to become involved in a violent gang-related confrontation. Not to mention there was an immediate defense-of-life situation with all of those families out trick or treating. The suspect began to chase the other two rival gang members down the sidewalk. Williams and Rosenberg continued to monitor this life-threatening situation. As the suspect ran adjacent to the St. Joseph's Student Residence, Williams drove up adjacent to the suspect, who was subsequently identified as Julio Moran. Believing Moran was armed with a fire-arm and about to shoot two rival gang members, he had been chasing towards a nearby alley, Rosenberg withdrew his Beretta 92F semi-automatic 9mm pistol, identified himself as a Los Angeles Police Officer, and ordered Moran to drop his weapon. This was an imminent defense of life situation.

Moran choose to ignore Rosenberg's lawful, verbal commands and instead, turned in the direction of Rosenberg and Williams pointing his extended arms with the towel wrapped around his hands in a threatening manner. Rosenberg, who was still seated in the front passenger's seat of their undercover vehicle, fear-ing for his life and for Williams fired several rounds from his 92F Beretta 9mm semi-automatic pistol in the direction of Moran, while continuing to verbally order Moran to drop his weapon.

Initially, it appeared Rosenberg's rounds had absolutely no affect upon Moran. Within seconds, Dave began reloading his weapon, as Moran still remained a threat. That's when Williams reached across Rosenberg while verbally order-ing Moran to drop his weapon. A second officer-involved-shooting occurred. Believing that Moran still posed an imminent threat to them, Williams fired several rounds from his Smith & Wesson 9mm semi-automatic pistol at Moran, who finally collapsed onto the sidewalk.

They simultaneously broadcasted, "Officer's needs help" and their location. Within minutes, numerous patrol units arrived. Keep in mind, this entire incident unfolded within seconds, two officer-involved shootings. One of the first responding officers was Police Officer II Henry "Hank" Cousine (RIP), who unwrapped the towel from around Moran's hands and discovered he was unarmed. Cousine was in the process of rendering first aide. Based on the total-ity of the circumstances, Rosenberg and Williams reaction during this deadly use of force was justified.

In the meantime, Los Angeles City Fire Department had been summoned to the location. Cousine and his partner began to establish the crime scene and canvass the immediate area for evidence and witnesses. That's when Cousine noticed a vehicle had driven by the location at least twice. An investigative stop was conducted, and it was determined that the occupants, all gang members, were Moran's homeboys. As paramedics rendered emergency medical assistance to Moran, Cousine convinced the occupants that detectives needed to interview them to get their statements for the investigation.

Surprisingly, they decided to cooperate and drove to Southwest Station to be interviewed. It was later confirmed that Moran had intentionally exited their vehicle to chase the two rival gang members into the nearby alley. The plan was once in the alley the two rival gang members would be shot Uzi once they entered the alley. Remember earlier in this book, I introduced you to the California Felony Murder Rule.

Moran was rushed to County USC Medical Center, where, unfortunately, he failed to respond to medical treatment. Moran's body was transferred to the Los Angeles County Coroner's Office, located at 1104 North Mission Road, Los Angeles.

Officer-Involved Shooting Protocol

As is customary with any officer-involved shooting, the process begins. The involved officer(s) are separated and ordered to provide a public safety statement to the first responding supervisor on-scene. This statement is required of the officer(s) under the proper circumstances and supersedes officer's rights to remain silent.

The public safety statement is required when there are outstanding suspects or there is the possibility of citizens being harmed or evidence being lost if information is withheld. Officers are appointed an attorney. There is attorney-client privilege, however, no such privilege exists between their employee representative relating to criminal acts by them or other officers. The attorney and employee representative are not there to change what occurred. Their jobs are to protect the officer's rights and assist them in articulating what happened and why they did what they did. Officers will never be told to change the facts.

Failing to tell the truth could result in being charged criminally. In addition to the administrative investigation relating to the incident, during this era, the Robbery Homicide Division, Officer-Involved Shooting Section were also responsible for investigating any actions that might be criminal or constitute misconduct.

Detectives from the Los Angeles Police Department's Robbery Homicide Division, Officer-Involved Shooting Section, interviewed Williams and Rosenberg. After being interviewed, they were placed on administrative leave and ordered to Behavioral Science Services (BSS) for counseling and evaluation. This provided the department with an expert's opinion as to an officer's fitness for return to duty and was part of the process for every officer-involved shooting.

The job of BSS was to advise the department about an officer's frame of mind as it related to their ability to perform their duties after a significant critical incident, especially a fatal officer-involved shooting. Rosenberg and Williams completed the aforementioned Officer-Involved Shooting Protocol.

Returned to Duty

(Officer-Involved Shooting Number Two)

On Wednesday, November 7, 1990, one week to the day of Rosenberg and Williams' officer-involved shooting, they returned to work cleared for field duty. Their shooting would eventually be presented to the Los Angeles County District Attorney's Office for review and adjudication. The Department's Use of Force Review Board would also convened to take a critical look at the involved officer's tactics before, during, and after the shooting, including the drawing and exhibiting of their firearms and whether the use of deadly force was in or out of policy.

Gang-Related Homicide

In any event, Rosenberg and Williams were back to work; so we decided to take them to Code 7, aka dinner. We dined at the local taco restaurant located in the strip mall on the corner of Figueroa and 30th streets. While breaking bread, Rosenberg and Williams discussed the details of their shooting. We finished eating our meals and were headed back to the station when Communications Division broadcasted: "Southwest Units handle this call first. Ambulance shooting just occurred in the parking lot of Pizza Hut located on Vermont Avenue and 36th Street."

We immediately responded to the shooting call. Upon our arrival, there were several uniformed officers already Code 6 at scene as well as paramedics from the Los Angeles City Fire Department, who were rendering emergency medical treatment to the victim, Timothy Campbell, aka Tim Stacks, an active member of the local Blood street gang. Unfortunately, Tim Stacks would not survive the shooting; he was pronounced *DRT* at the scene. Further investigation disclosed Tim Stacks' vehicle had been stolen during the commission of his murder. Rosenberg had built a rapport with an associate of the decedent's street gang. I don't think Tim Stack's murder was more than 20 minutes old before Rosenberg received a telephone call from that contact, who disclosed several of the decedent's homeboys were gearing up to do a payback shooting.

According to Rosenberg's contact, those gang members were identified as Dennis Johnson, Melvin Kidd, and Marcus Dupree. They were armed with semi-automatic firearms and rolling in a white Chevrolet Nova from the 1100 block of 37th Street.

Homicide Investigation Underway

Homicide Detectives assigned to Southwest Detectives were notified and had responded to the crime scene. Homicide Detective Coordinator, Detective III John Bunch, Detective II Gil Freese, and Detective II Rick Marks had responded to handle the homicide investigation. After Rosenberg received the information, we drove back to the station, checked out two shotguns and tacked up in our ballistic vest and LAPD raid jackets to be clearly identifiable. That night, I was driving a brand new 1990; blue Ford four-door, Crown Victoria dual-purpose police vehicle.

The vehicle had been loaned to me by one of the day watch detectives, PJ Jones, after I promised that I would take good care of it. That meant I was responsible for ensuring the interior was clean, for filling up the vehicle's gas tank at end of watch and for avoiding any unnecessary vehicle damage.

Stolen Vehicle Following and Arrests

Based on the information Rosenberg received, we concentrated our enforcement efforts in the Bloods' territory. I recalled driving; Ray Marquez was seated in the front seat, Williams and Rosenberg seated in the rear passenger's seats.

Williams was seated behind me, and Rosenberg was seated directly behind Marquez. I remember I was driving westbound on 37th Street from Catalina Street when we observed a late '80s Buick Regal being driven and occupied by two young Black males. We began to follow them, Ray requested DMV and auto status of the vehicle license plate. The driver made a left turn into the driveway of a nearby residence.

I stopped our police vehicle just east and recalled telling Ray, Dave, and Don that if the two men exited their vehicle and walked toward the resident's front door, we would move on. All of a sudden, we saw reverse taillights, and the suspect's vehicle began to back out of the driveway. We were still awaiting a return on the plate. In the meantime, we were now following the vehicle westbound on 37th Place toward Normandie Avenue.

Ray updated Communications Division of our location. We were stopped for the red tri-light signal northbound Normandie Avenue at Jefferson Boulevard, in the number one lane of traffic. The tri-light signal changed, and we continued to follow the vehicle, passing 30th Street still northbound on Normandie Avenue.

While following the suspect's vehicle, we discussed tactics and how we would respond if the suspects were armed or decided to run. The vehicle made another quick left turn onto 27th Street from Normandie Avenue. Finally, Communications Division advised us that the vehicle had been reported stolen. We broadcasted our location and requested two marked black and white police vehicles, as well as, an air unit.

In the meantime, the suspect's vehicle made a quick right into the north/south alley heading north and attempted to negotiate another quick left turn into an east/west alley heading west. The suspect's vehicle was rapidly entering another Blood Street gang's neighborhood. Luckily for us, they were unable to navigate the alley due to numerous parked vehicles obstructing the alley.

We took full advantage of their bad luck and were able to take them into custody without incident. The suspects—juveniles—were placed into the back seat of our police vehicle to be transported back to the station for booking. We made a command decision to have Rosenberg follow us back to the station in the stolen vehicle. Our plan was to expedite the booking process of the juveniles.

Gangster's Payback Shooting

Later, on our way back to the station, we were traveling southbound on Normandie Avenue at 30th Street with the juveniles in our custody, and Rosenberg was following us in the stolen vehicle. Communications Division broadcasted: "Southwest Units. Shots fired in the area of Denker Avenue and Exposition Boulevard. Suspects were last seen driving northbound from the location in a white compact vehicle armed with semi-automatic weapons."

Marquez, Williams, and I all acknowledged the shooting had to be the payback, especially because it had occurred in Crip territory. We continued driving southbound on Normandie Avenue approaching 36th Street. As we began to enter the intersection for north/south traffic, a white Chevrolet Nova driving eastbound ran the mid-phase red tri-light signal on 36th Street. There were three male adult Blacks in the vehicle. There was absolutely no doubt; those were the suspects involved in the shooting. More importantly, Rosenberg's contact had provided reliable information.

Pop Quiz: So what would you do? You are transporting two juveniles to the station from the stolen vehicle caper. One of your partners is driving the stolen vehicle back to the station to expedite things. Should you?

A. Contact Communications Division about your observations and ignore the suspects.

B. Immediately follow the suspects' vehicle, which you believe was involved in the shooting.

C. Release the juveniles and pursue the shooting suspects.

D. Both B and C

If you selected A, you're crazy! Even though that would have been the correct answer. However, on that particular night, we were gunslingers and selected B. Our decision on that night would definitely come back later to haunt us. In any event, we were paid to track down and take gangsters into custody, especially shooters, who thought it was OK and normal to shoot up neighborhoods and innocent victims.

I made a left turn eastbound onto 36th Street from Normandie Avenue and accelerated to catch up with the suspect's vehicle, which, by this time, had made a right turn onto Catalina Street and then a quick left onto 37th Place. The suspect's vehicle stopped in front of 1137 West 37th Place. Marquez broadcasted our location as I simultaneously activated the forward-facing red light.

In-Vehicle Pursuit

By this time, the suspect's vehicle had rapidly accelerated eastbound toward Vermont Avenue and then turned right onto southbound Vermont Avenue driving toward the active crime scene on Vermont Avenue at 36th Street. It was obvious these suspects had no intention of pulling over or complying with the law. We continued southbound until we reached Exposition Boulevard where the suspect's vehicle made a right turn.

Normally the front passenger was responsible for broadcasting the pursuit. Williams, who was seated in the backseat with the juveniles, took the mic from Marquez and started screaming into it. Even I had difficulty understanding what he was saying. Rosenberg, being a good partner, was following us in the pursuit in the stolen vehicle. This was a classic caper. As the suspects reached Normandie Avenue, they made a right turn onto northbound Normandie Avenue. They continued until they reached 37th Street again, where they made a right turn, heading eastbound once again. When they reached Catalina Street, they made a right turn and then a quick left onto 37th Drive, which was a dead-end cul-de-sac. The only way out was to drive up on the grass onto the sidewalk and back onto Vermont Avenue.

By this time, the driver, now identified as Dennis Johnson, began to open up the driver's door as if he was going to jump out of the moving vehicle. The next thing I know, Marquez opened his front passenger door. I yelled out to him to shut the door. I told Marquez, "If the suspect jumps out of the vehicle, I'm going to run his ass over!" These were armed and dangerous suspects, and I was not about to allow him to get a free shot off on my partners and me. As we followed the suspect's vehicle up onto the grassy area at the end of the cul-de-sac, Marquez still had his passenger's door slightly ajar and while driving over the grass onto the sidewalk, it struck the parking meter. Now, I'm pissed. All I could think was, "Damn, Detective PJ Jones is not going to loan us his vehicle anymore." I wasn't worried about the suspects at this point of the pursuit. I was a little pissed off at Marquez for opening the damn door.

Officer-Involved Shooting No. 90-137

The Assistant Watch Commander, Sergeant II Pam Roberts asked me, "What is it about you guys and Wednesday nights?" I replied, "Ma'am, welcome to the Wild Southwest!"

The suspects were now headed southbound on Vermont Avenue toward the active crime scene for a second time. Rosenberg was still behind us in the stolen vehicle. By this time, Detective Freese had directed Rosenberg to pull over and park the stolen vehicle on the northwest corner of Vermont Avenue at Exposition Boulevard. The suspect turned right again onto northbound Normandie

Avenue and then right onto eastbound 37th Street. Once the suspects reached Catalina Street, they turned left onto 37th Place.

By this time, the suspect's vehicle slowed and Melvin Kidd jumped out of the rear passenger side. Detective Marks ran down the sidewalk, and then we heard a single gunshot and Marks fell to the ground. Believing that Kidd had just shot Marks, Williams bailed out of the backseat of our police vehicle. Meanwhile, Marquez and I—still with the two juveniles—continued pursuing Dennis Johnson and the other suspect, Marcus Dupree. When Johnson's vehicle approached Raymond Avenue, he made a quick right turn and drove into the east/west alley north of 37th Street.

Marquez updated Communications Division of our location, as I drove into the alley. We instructed the juveniles to duck down in their seats. The alley was so full of dust; I thought we were driving through the dust bowl. Approximately 30 yards into the alley, I observed taillights ahead of us. Marquez and I had already deployed our firearms, 92F Beretta semi-automatic pistols.

All of a sudden, I observed this silhouette run between the rear of the suspect's vehicle, about seven yards in front of our vehicle. I pointed my firearm, prepared to engage the suspect, it was Dennis Johnson; he was unarmed. I watched as he began to climb over a nearby chain-link fence. Johnson was proned out at gunpoint and taken into custody without further incident. Obviously, it was his lucky night. Trust me when I say that!

By this time, Air 12 was overhead coordinating the large perimeter for containment. They advised Communications Division that all outstanding suspects had been taken into custody. However, our main concern centered on the health of brother officer, Detective Marks. We received good news: Marks was OK and had not been shot. It was later determined that while in foot pursuit, Marks had deployed his weapon to engage Suspect Melvin Kidd. Unfortunately, he lost his balance after stumbling on the sidewalk, causing him to fall. The impact caused his firearm to discharge.

In the meantime, a loaded firearm and U.S. currency was located concealed inside of Dennis Johnson's vehicle during the inventory search by investigators. Outstanding suspect Marcus Dupree managed to elude capture that night, however, he was arrested several days later. The Assistant Watch Commander, Sergeant II Pam Roberts asked me, "What is it about you guys and Wednesday nights?" I replied, "Pam, welcome to the Wild Southwest!"

Well, after that shooting incident, I'm sure management viewed the Drive-by Shooting Team as a civil liability as opposed to a benefit. Lieutenant Kerstein made the decision, for his peace of mind, to disband our unit. I remained assigned to detectives. However, Don, Dave, Ray, and Memo were all reassigned to patrol.

Although, I was not directly involved as a shooter in the officer-involved shooting, the entire caper was investigated as one occurrence. Like I mentioned earlier, our actions would come back to haunt us. As a result of giving the juveniles a free scared straight tour of duty, our tactics were frowned upon, and we received additional training. It was a catch-22 situation: we had observed shooters, had two juveniles in custody, and had to make a quick decision. It was all a part of the learning process. We all survived, and the suspects were taken into custody, DR No. 90-03-00695.

Appointment to Detective Trainee
Southwest Detective Division

On January 3, 1991, all my hard work paid off. I interviewed and was selected for the permanent Detective Trainee position at Southwest Detective Division. This was a really big deal. In fact, my wife received this letter of congratulations signed by Area Commanding Officer, Captain III Garrett W. Zimmon and Lieutenant Kerstein, Commanding Officer, Southwest Detective Division.

February 27, 1991

Dear Winifred Landrum:

Now that Mo has been assigned to the position of Detective Trainee, I thought I would let you know how he was selected for the job.

We take great care in the process of selecting those who are assigned to our detectives here. When we had an opening for Detective Trainee, we looked for a Police Officer who had, (1) an outstanding reputation; (2) was gifted with certain abilities; and (3) who had the qualities and abilities to promote within the Department.

Police Officers who fit the category were interviewed, and Mo came out as the best candidate. You should be very proud of this achievement; it's a big career step.

We consider his assignment to Detectives as a promotion. Promotion in LAPD does not come easy. It requires hard work and dedication. Officers must set goals early in their careers and then work odd hours, untold overtime, and thankless positions before they can achieve success. Mo has done it. I realize, that the success was not his alone. Without a loving, dedicated wife such as you, Mo's achievements would have been a lot harder, if not impossible. Therefore, you too deserve to share in the credit.

Now you would think, I would get relieved from honey do's. Not so fast, it was business as usual within the Landrum's household. By this time, my loving wife was a Los Angeles County Deputy Sheriff.

CHAPTER 17

Rodney King Incident

A significant incident occurred on March 3, 1991, the infamous vehicle pursuit initiated by the California Highway Patrol Officers Tim and Melanie Singer. At some point, the Los Angeles Police Department was contacted for assistance. Sergeant Stacey Koon, along with Los Angeles Police Officers, Laurence Powell, Timothy Wind, Theodore Briseno, and Rolando Solano responded to the termination point. They were all assigned to Foothill Patrol Division.

At the termination point of the vehicle pursuit, a civilian (George Holliday) used his video camera to videotape what transpired. A violent use of force occurred. Holliday, disturbed by what he had observed, went to Foothill Patrol Division and wanted to give his video recording to a desk officer that night. We were told by several anonymous sources that the desk officer and watch commander kicked Holliday out of the station instead of procuring the video recording. Holliday went to the local news media, which not only accepted his video recording; but also disseminated it to every major news media outlet for months.

The *Los Angeles Times* joined in and wrote dozens of news articles. It was like watching a mini series except this was real life. The fallout resulted in criminal charges being filed against Sergeant Koon, and officers Powell, Wind, and Briseno. The trial venue was changed from Los Angeles County to Ventura County and held in Simi Valley, California. On April 29, 1992, the verdicts were read: Sergeant Koon and the officers were all found not guilty.

The verdict definitely ignited the entire city of Los Angeles, which resulted in widespread civil unrest, aka rioting, shootings, and looting. The Los Angeles Riots were the deadliest in Los Angeles' history. There were approximately 63 murders from April 29 through May 4, 1992. This single incident resulted in the Los Angeles City Council meeting, adopting, and passing new legislation called the "Charter F Amendment." Basically, it established term limits for future mayors, councilpersons and the chief of police. During this turbulent time, Mayor Tom Bradley and Chief Daryl F. Gates were not seeing eye-to-eye. In the meantime, Koon and Powell faced federal civil rights violations and criminal charges.

They would both be convicted and sentenced to 30 months in federal prison. Sergeant Koon, Powell, Wind, and Briseno were all terminated as employees of the Los Angeles Police Department. During April 1992, I was assigned to South Bureau Homicide.

Christopher Commission List

As a direct result of the Rodney King Incident and public outcry, an Independent Commission was formed to investigate bias, prejudice, racism, and excessive use of force incidents involving LAPD officers. Mr. Warren Minor Christopher, a lawyer, former diplomat and politician, headed up the Independent Commission, known as the Christopher Commission. The commission reviewed and analyzed data obtained from internal LAPD resources, such as reportable uses of force and personnel complaint histories of LAPD officers. There were also several town hall meetings held in which the public provided input, (i.e., complained, about particular officers within their communities).

Whether you agree or not, the commission did its job, however, no officers, including me, were ever given an opportunity to speak before the Christopher Commission. I was listed as number 20 on the list of 44 officers. I met separately with two deputy chiefs to ascertain the criteria for being placed on the list; neither one could answer the question. I made the list for reporting my uses of force. Please allow me to repeat that: I made the list of 44 for reporting my uses of force. Not for reporting excessive force, but for being honest. I was a pro-aggressive police officer, who was involved in pro-active police work on a nightly basis. If you remember, I was suspended for seven days while assigned to West Bureau CRASH for failure to report a use of force. So, its damned if you do, and damned if you don't!

During one of the many town hall meetings held at Jim Gilliam's Park, located in Southwest Patrol Division, it came as no surprise to me that gang members from a particular Blood street gang attended and complained —snitched—on me. Now imagine that gangsters snitching, say it isn't so! Earlier I indicated, "We were Violent Men for Violent Times and so were the Gangsters." That was a true and accurate statement. During my tour of duty in Southwest Patrol Division, I arrested numerous armed, and dangerous felons.

When it came time to take some of them into custody, a great majority of them refused to comply with my lawful, verbal commands, directions and orders. Their outright refusal to comply prompted me to respond to their defiance by the use of force necessary to overcome their aggressive and combative resistance. I used the tools and techniques we were taught in the Los Angeles Police Academy.

Gang-related Shooting In Progress
Crips vs. Bloods

What if you're out with your senior partner conducting a follow-up, and you observe a shooting-in-progress, two suspects firing into the courtyard of an occupied apartment complex with semi-automatic weapons. What would you do? Well, this is a true story of such an incident!

On Friday, November 8, 1991, I was assigned to Southwest Night Watch Detectives with my partner, Detective I Neal May. We were dressed in slacks, dress shirts, and ties conducting a follow-up on a crime report in The Jungle. I was driving our dual-purpose police vehicle, traveling southbound on Hillcrest Drive from Martin Luther King Boulevard. It was between 10 and 11 p.m., so there was little pedestrian traffic out during those hours. It was cold, a little breezy and the street was illuminated by several overhanging mercury vapor streetlights.

Before Neal and I would reached Santa Rosalia Drive, the next major street south of Martin Luther King Boulevard, we observed a small pick-up truck double-parked in front of 3907 Hillcrest Drive, aka Town and Country Apartments just north of us. The occupants suddenly began firing multiple rounds into the courtyard. This was not a movie; we were witnessing a shooting in progress. Only in the Wild Southwest!

Neal and I began to talk tactics. I decided it would be in our best interest to position our vehicle in a northwesterly direction to engage the suspects, who by this time were driving southbound rapidly on Hillcrest Drive toward Santa Rosalia Drive. Neal advised Communications Division of our observations and location. As the suspects reached Santa Rosalia Drive, we observed two Black male adults inside the cabin of the pick-up—a Chevrolet S-10 pick-up truck with Oregon license plates.

Vehicle Pursuit of Shooting Suspects

We began to follow the suspects, who suddenly accelerated at a high speed away from us. Neal advised Communications Division that we were now in vehicle pursuit of drive-by shooting suspects. As I drove north on Santa Rosalia Drive toward Coliseum Street, the suspects' vehicle made a sharp right turn onto east-bound Coliseum Street, heading back toward Martin Luther King Boulevard.

I could hear units en route to our call for assistance, sirens and the whole nine, as well as, an air unit, just minutes out. The suspects ran the red tri-light signal at the intersection of Coliseum Street and Martin Luther King Boulevard.

We cleared the same intersection, still in vehicle pursuit of the suspects. As the suspects reached the Y-intersection at Coliseum Street and Chesapeake Avenue, the driver attempted to negotiate a sharp left turn, which caused the vehicle to turn over onto the passenger's side. Neal updated Communications Division about what had just occurred. We bailed out of our police vehicle immediately and took cover behind our doors; firearms deployed, and aimed in the direction of the shooter' vehicle ready and prepared to engage them. Additional units were still en route to our Code 6 location.

"Please Don't Shoot Him!"

We were stopped approximately 40 yards south of the suspect's vehicle, when suddenly both suspect's heads popped up. They hopped out of the driver's side window and began to split up. Now, if it had been two officers in an overturned vehicle, they would have been seriously injured. Only suspects survive freaking stuff like that.

In any event, the passenger ran in an easterly direction, as the driver ran away in a northwesterly direction. I focused in on the driver, who was holding his waistband, I began to sight in on him when I heard Neal say, "Mo, please don't shoot him!" Neal had just interviewed for a detective position with Robbery Homicide Division and was being strongly considered. I understood his concern, but this suspect needed to be stopped.

As the suspect approached the wrought iron security gate of the Woodlake Manor Apartment complex and began to climb over the gate, the loaded Uzi pistol he had attempted to conceal in his waistband fell to the ground. My instincts were correct, but I did not drop him because Neal had begged me not to. If any suspect deserved to be stopped by all means necessary, it was Mr. Uzi.

The Uzi was recovered, and a large-scale perimeter was set up. Thanks to the help of numerous responding officers as well as the assistance of Metropolitan Division's K-9 units and Air Support Division, both suspects were eventually located and taken into custody without incident. The Chevrolet S-10 pick-up truck had been entered into the system as, "armed and dangerous." It had been taken the day before during the commission of a robbery/homicide in Wilshire Patrol Division. The owner of the truck had been robbed and murdered in the parking lot of a local hotel by a Black male adult armed with an Uzi-type weapon. Numerous units responded to our original crime scene at the Town and Country Apartments and miraculously no one there had been shot, but there was plenty of evidence to be collected.

The suspects were both Crip gang members from two separate criminal street gangs within Wilshire Patrol Division. The location that had been shot up was a known hangout for a local Southwest-area Blood street gang. The suspects were eventually charged and convicted of robbery and murder. The Uzi-carrying suspect was sentenced to life without parole. I could have saved our taxpayers a boatload of money if Neal would have allowed me to take care of business on November 8, 1991!

In any event, my thanks to Neal and the numerous police officers that responded that night, we were able to apprehend two violent predators and remove them from the community. In January 1992, I was loaned out to South Bureau Homicide where, within a couple months, I would be officially transferred.

Commendations
Southwest Patrol Division

08/08/1986	COMMENDATION
Officer Landrum, you are commended for participation in firearm tactics training day for line and technical reserve officers.	
09/22/1986	COMMENDATION
Officer Landrum, you are commended for dedication and attention to duty as well as observations skills, knowledge, teamwork, command presence and professionalism resulting in the arrest of an escaped felon.	
10/16/1986	COMMENDATION
Officer Landrum, you are to be commended for best overall recap during Deployment Period 10—outstanding and exemplary. Commended for diligence and attention to duty.	
01/20/1987	COMMENDATION
Officer Landrum, you are to be commended for your attention and dedication to duty, professionalism and performance under stress, tactics, teamwork, and execution.	

02/04/1987	COMMENDATION

Officer Landrum, you are to be commended by ABC, Inc. Security Supervisor for total attention to duty during the 1987 American Music Awards. Also commended for displaying the highest professionalism.

03/10/1987	COMMENDATION

Officer Landrum, you are to be commended for outstanding tactical planning and implementation of surveillance and arrest procedure that led to the arrest of seven persons and the recovery of drugs and a loaded firearm.

03/17/1987	COMMENDATION

Officer Landrum, you are to be commended for your attention to duty, patrol tactics, and investigative/interrogation techniques that led to arrest for California Penal Code, Section 487.3-Grand Theft Auto.

04/14/1987	COMMENDATION

Officer Landrum, you are commended by Narcotics Division for support during a successful Narcotics Task Force during February 12, 13, & 14, 1987. Also commended for your perseverance and dedication.

06/05/1987	COMMENDATION

Officer Landrum, you are to be commended for your efforts, dedication, and attention to duty, sound judgment, tactics and performance during a divisional narcotics sweep.

08/07/1987	COMMENDATION

Officer Landrum, you are to be commended for a job well done in the arrest of five "Coyote" for kidnapping a 15-year-old child. The case was solid and all suspects pled guilty. Great Police Work!

10/14/1987	COMMENDATION

Officer Landrum, you are to be commended for your quick response, through preliminary investigation and keen observation skills that led to the arrest of a potentially dangerous felon.

01/06/1988	COMMENDATION

Officer Landrum, you are to be commended for your attention to duty, knowledge of crime problem and investigation resulting in arrest of felon.

01/29/1988	COMMENDATION

Officer Landrum, you are to be commended for the arrest of three armed suspects within 35 minutes after the crime. Astute observation and patrol tactics that led to great arrests.

02/19/1988	COMMENDATION

Officer Landrum, you are to be commended for your concern and support of a member of the LAPD Family. "There is no greater call to service than responding to an Officer who needs help." Thank you for your concern and support for an officer accidentally shot by their 4-year-old daughter. You and other officers raised $1,000.

03/03/1988	COMMENDATION

Officer Landrum, you are to be commended for your initiative, attention to duty, and resourcefulness in the arrest and removal of a dangerous person from the streets of Los Angeles, resulting in attempted murder charges being filed against him.

03/10/1988	COMMENDATION

Officer Landrum, you are to be commended for your commendatory performance during the visit of Pope John Paul II, dedication to duty, loyalty to Department, tireless effort, and outstanding uniform appearance.

03/14/1988	COMMENDATION

Officer Landrum, you are to be commended for your attention to duty, observation skills, and thorough investigation, which resulted in the timely return of stolen property and the arrest of a burglary suspect.

03/16/1988	COMMENDATION
Officer Landrum, you are to be commended for your attention to duty, initiative, and tactics that led to arrest of suspect involved in shots fired from a shotgun. Also commended for good report writing.	
05/13/1988	COMMENDATION
Officer Landrum, you are to be commended during Deployment Period No. 4, 1988. Distinguished for answering police calls for service, preliminary investigations as well as initiating traffic stops and arrests.	
06/21/1998	COMMENDATION
Officer Landrum, you are to be commended for your participation in Operation Slam Dunk for your narcotics investigative expertise, knowledge in the area of search warrant preparation, dedication to duty, and tactics.	
06/27/1988	COMMENDATION
Officer Landrum, Neighborhood Watch thanked you for your admiration and fine work in closing down a dope house on Jefferson Boulevard, making the community safer.	
06/30/1988	COMMENDATION
Officer Landum, Southwest SPU commends you for being well trained and supervised. Officers commended for outstanding field tactics, safety skills, and teamwork resulting in the arrest of narcotic traffickers.	
07/13/1998	COMMENDATION
Chief Rathburn note with commendation for SPU accomplishment with "Any Time Any Place" motto. Gang Task Force reduced crime and danger in the community.	

10/11/1989	COMMENDATION

Officer Landrum, you are to be commended for your teamwork, observation skills, and command presence that led to the successful arrest of potentially dangerous suspect armed with a gun without incident. Congratulations on a job well done!

02/23/1989	COMMENDATION

Officer Landrum, you are to be commended for your swift action and excellent work that stopped a dangerous criminal who cleared 32 burglaries in the Leimert Park area. Great initiative, teamwork, and M.O. knowledge.

03/30/1989	COMMENDATION

Letter of thanks and admiration for quick thinking and good retention of stolen rental auto information that led to recovery and arrest for Grand Theft Auto.

04/03/1989	COMMENDATION

Officer Landrum, you are to be commended for attention and dedication to duty and superior investigate techniques, which resulted in the arrest of hardcore Rollin 30 gang member for robbery.

04/13/1989	COMMENDATION

Officer Landrum, you are to be commended for attention and dedication to duty, investigative expertise, and superior interview techniques that led to arrest of robbery suspect.

06/20/1989	COMMENDATION

Officer Landrum, you are to be commended for your attention to duty, knowledge of the criminals in the area, which resulted in the arrest of a grand theft auto suspect.

06/27/1989	COMMENDATION

Officer Landrum, you are to be commended for being one of the top "producers" on PM Watch for Deployment Period No. 6, 1989.

07/13/1989	COMMENDATION
Officer Landrum, you are to be commended for your keen observation skills and quick reaction to armed robbery in progress that led to arrest of two armed robbery suspects.	
07/27/1989	COMMENDATION
Officer Landrum, you are to be commended for your quick response and outstanding report writing that led to felony filing on an intimidating a witness suspect.	
08/21/1989	COMMENDATION
Officer Landrum, you are to be commended for your observation and recall skills, knowledge of felony suspects and gang members, tactical skills, and planning that led to the arrest of an assault-with-a-deadly weapon suspect.	
12/31/1989	COMMENDATION
Assisted Gang Task Force used outstanding teamwork, professionalism, and dedication above and beyond the call of duty in enforcement against gangs.	
01/18/1990	CLASS "D" COMMENDATION
Awarded Class D Commendation for receipt of six commendations in a one-year period: 04/13/1989, 06/20/1989, 06/27/1989, 07/13/1989, 07/27/1989, and 08/21/1989.	
07/11/1990	COMMENDATION
Officer Landrum, you are to be commended your interest, knowledge, dedicated teamwork, incredible recall, attention to detail, and energetic commitment in arrest for 664/187 attempted murder of two victims.	

07/20/1989	COMMENDATION FROM: DEPUTY CHIEF WILLIAM RATHBURN

Detective Trainee Landrum, you are highly commended for attention to duty, teamwork, observation skills, interview skills, and diligence in bringing this tragic incident to a successful conclusion. Resulting in the arrest of four suspects in the attempted murder of a two-year-old child.

08/22/1990	COMMENDATION

Detective Trainee Landrum, you are to be commended for investigative skills and tenacity in difficult drive-by shooting cases, perservance, and success in arrests for six attempted murder drive-by suspects.

10/18/1990	COMMENDATION

Detective Trainee Landrum, you are to be commended for initial rape investigation of two USC female students. Highly commended for outstanding investigative skills, exceptional teamwork, planning abilities, and arrest of suspect who had fled to Pomona, California.

10/29/1990	COMMENDATION

Commended by USC for quick apprehension of rape suspect who terrorized USC neighborhood, hard work, dedication, and successful investigation.

12/23/1990	COMMENDATION

Detective Trainee Landrum, you are to be commended for your attention to duty, outstanding investigative technique that led to good arrest and conviction for attempted murder, Great Police Work!

01/15/1991	COMMENDATION

Detective Trainee Landrum, you are to be commended for tenacity, investigative perseverance, interview techniques, and compassion with victim's parents and reluctant witnesses, led to arrest to attempt murder.

01/17/1991	COMMENDATION

Thank you for perfect attendance during 1990 and good health, which speaks highly of your loyalty and devotion to duty.

05/02/1991	COMMENDATION

Outstanding recollection of suspect identities and monikers, teamwork, and spirit of cooperation, led to six felony arrests of kidnap, rape, lewd conduct suspects.

11/08/1991	COMMENDATION

Dedication, teamwork, and quality investigation that led to arrest of two very dangerous and active robbery criminals also wanted for murder.

11/15/1991	COMMENDATION

Detective Trainee Landrum, you are to be commended for hard work, initiative, expertise, and concern for citizens of Southwest Investigation and arrest of shooter near high school.

12/17/1991	COMMENDATION

Detective Trainee Landrum you have been nominated for the American Legion Award as the 1992 Detective Division Nominee for your continuing contribution to the citizens of Southwest Area.

01/06/1992	COMMENDATION

Commended for your outstanding effort to use no sick time in 1991. Attendance and good health reflect proudly on your loyalty and devotion to duty.

CHAPTER 18

South Bureau Homicide

(OUR MOTTO: Our day begins when your day ends!)

On March 22, 1992, I was officially transferred to South Bureau Homicide (SBH), located at 4125 South Crenshaw Boulevard, Los Angeles. The Commanding Officer-In-Charge was Lieutenant II Sergio Robelto (R.I.P.). When I think about leadership, Lieutenant Robelto's name immediately comes to mind, without a doubt. SBH had been centralized and designed to handle all homicides that occurred within South Bureau. In 1992, unfortunately, it was one of busiest, if not the busiest homicide unit, in the United States. During 1992, SBH alone investigated approximately 492 murders.

There were approximately 70 detectives assigned, and every one of us had a caseload. I had only been assigned to SBH for a month before the Rodney King not guilty verdicts. As I mentioned earlier, the Los Angeles Riots were deadly and costly. My training officer Detective II Chuck Hawley was an outstanding homicide investigator, thorough and a skilled interrogator. Hawley trained me well. It did not take long before we were assigned our first homicide case as partners.

The murder investigation that I am about to describe occurred on the last day of the Los Angeles Riots. During the course of this homicide investigation, we used numerous department resources at our disposal, pulling out all the stops to bring the vicious predators to justice.

Michelle Helford Murder Investigation

(Spin the Bottle Rape/Murder)

Monday, May 4, 1992, Hawley and I were seated at our respective desks in SBH. Detective Coordinator Paul Mize informed us that we were first up in the rotation for any homicide notifications within South Bureau. Approximately 10 minutes later, the Southeast Watch Commander contacted SBH about a homicide that Hawley and I would be assigned to handle. I directed one of our clerical staff members to query the ACC computer for the Southeast homicide incident. She procured the print out for me that described the discovery of a White female lying in the north/south alley between 98th and 97th streets, east of Broadway. Hawley and I drove to the location, which had been cordoned off by Southeast Patrol Division officers to establish the crime scene. We signed in on the crime scene log and informed the officers we were the assigned SBH detectives for this particular homicide investigation. Although the alley had been cordoned off prior to our arrival, there were numerous curious onlookers standing just outside of the crime scene tape.

The Investigation

Several feet away from where the decedent's body was discovered there was an occupied residence. Hawley and I knocked on the door and spoke to the occupants inside, who disclosed they heard gunshots around 1 a.m., but thought nothing of it, because gunshots in their neighborhood occurred so frequently. According to them, they heard shots only and did not see anything.

Often, when canvassing crime scenes this was the standard response. Unfortunately, many citizens living within the community, including in Watts where this homicide took place, were afraid to come forward due to fear of retaliation. We were fully aware and understood their concerns. This was going to be what we often referred to in homicide as a, "Who-Done-It Caper!"

Neighborhood Canvass

Several other detectives had responded and were canvassing the immediate area for potential eyewitnesses and evidence. Although this was May 1992, we still looked for point, tilt, and zoom surveillance cameras. We also contacted other department resources to determine if there were any pole cameras installed nearby. We had no such luck with those endeavors. In any event, the Los Angeles County Coroner was notified to respond and conduct there on scene investigation.

Los Angeles County Coroner Investigator Notification

As a Homicide Investigator, one of my assigned functions was to contact the Los Angeles County Coroner's Office to obtain a coroner's case number. Once the preliminary field investigation was completed, the decedent's body was removed from the crime scene. In this particular case, the Los Angeles County Coroner's Investigator was contacted. Upon their arrival to the scene, the Coroner Investigator began to examine the decedent's lifeless body for signs of trauma and identification. So far, we had a youthful-looking deceased White female, wearing a pair of blue denim jeans with what appeared to be a pair of black lace panties stuffed and partially protruding from the back of her jeans.

There were several expended firearm casings surrounding the decedent's body. In fact, I saw that the victim was wearing a .45 caliber bullet necklace around her neck. Those casings were marked, photographed, and collected as evidence. The Coroner Investigator's investigation confirmed that the decedent had been shot numerous times in the upper torso and had one gunshot wound to her head. It was also determined that the black lace panties appeared to have been forcibly removed from the decedent. The Coroner's Investigator did not locate any type of identification on the decedent's person or in her personal effects. A Polaroid photograph of the decedent's face was taken and provided to me. The decedent's body was wrapped in clean plastic, placed in a body bag, and loaded onto the gurney to be transported to 1104 North Mission Road, Los Angeles. Among the onlookers, I recalled talking to a young, Hispanic female approximately eight or nine years old, who asked me, "Are you trying to find out where that lady lived?" I replied, "Yes, do you know where she lives." She replied, "Yes, down the street on 98th!" She pointed, and directed me to 120 West 98th Street.

Victim Positively Identified

I door knocked the residence at 120 West 98th Street. The door opened, and a female, Hispanic, subsequently identified as, P. Mendoza, stood in the doorway. I explained to Mendoza that I was assigned to South Bureau Homicide, currently investigating the death of a young White female. I told Mendoza that during the course of my investigation, I had been directed to contact the occupants of her residence to determine if they could positively identify the victim.

I showed the Polaroid photograph of the decedent to Mendoza, who immediately broke down and started crying. Mendoza responded, "Oh my God, that's Michelle!" I asked Mendoza if Michelle had a last name, and she replied, "Yes, Helford." I continued to interview Mendoza, who disclosed that Helford had run away from a foster home in the city of Rancho Cucamonga, and the last time she saw Helford alive was the night before.

Murder Suspects in Plain View

Here's some information that you may find disturbing: While interviewing Mendoza in her front yard, the three assholes responsible for the murder of Michelle Helford were close by. I recalled looking at two male Hispanics, subsequently identified via their gang monikers as, Sugar Bear and Pirate. They were loitering about in the front yard of the home just east of Mendoza's residence. The third suspect, subsequently identified as Shadow, walked up westbound on 98th Street from Main Street. I recalled Shadow's conversation with Mendoza like it was yesterday. Shadow was smoking a cigarette, and Mendoza asked him when was the last time he saw Michelle. Shadow replied, "The last time I saw Michelle was about 7 last night. I gave her a cigarette, then I went home!" I continued to gather as much information as possible from Mendoza. During our initial interview, Mendoza seemed genuinely concerned and shocked regarding Helford's brutal murder.

Comparing Notes & Making Notifications

Hawley and I returned to SBH to organize our murder book, compare notes, and complete the death report, then notified the Coroner's Investigator that we had a name for the murder victim. We discovered the victim was only 15 years old. We were awaiting a callback from the Coroner's Office so that I could attend Helford's autopsy, which would determine the official cause of death. When working homicide, it was important to keep in mind that the body was evidence, and will reveal exactly what happened to it. As a Homicide Investigator, it was our job to gather the evidence, find the truth, and bring those responsible for the heinous crime to justice.

Autopsy- Official Cause of Death

On Friday, May 1, 1992, Hawley and I were en route to the Los Angeles County Coroner's Office, one of the largest coroner's offices in the United States. It was going to be my first-ever autopsy, aka a forensic medical examination. Helford's autopsy was an experience that I would remember for the rest of my life. Several of my colleagues had suggested that I purchase a pair of Ray Ban sunglasses and some Vick's Vapor Rub to help minimize the odor of formaldehyde from the hundreds of dead bodies being stored in the crypt at the coroner's office. I would learn rather quickly that Vick's Vapor Rub only enhanced the smell! Laugh out loud!

Upon our arrival, Hawley and I entered through the coroner's intake area, signed in and immediately went into an adjacent room to put on protective scrubs over our clothing as well as a pair of shoe booties before entering the medical examination room. Imagine numerous gurneys lined up along the wall with dead bodies of every race, creed, and sexual orientation, all awaiting their autopsy. I recall that both examination rooms were open and bodies—in different stages of post-mortem—lay out on every available metal examination table. The entire experience seemed surreal. It was so busy; Hawley and I had to wait for coroner personnel to remove the body of an unrelated female decedent, who appeared to have been involved in some type of traffic collision.

I'll never forget that when they began to transfer her body from the examination table onto a gurney her entire right arm, which had apparently been severed from her body, just remained on the examination table.

Unfortunately, I had seen dozens and dozens of dead bodies while responding to homicide scene working patrol, but observing the process at the coroner's office was all new for me. After the examination table was cleared, the body of our victim was wheeled into the examination room. Her nude, lifeless body was placed on the examination table to be examined. The attending DME walked into the room, introduced himself, and began his examination. As mentioned earlier, the body is evidence and will provide you with a story of what happened to it. It was up to the DME to provide us with an official cause of death. The DME began by documenting all injuries, wounds, scars, and tattoos on Helford's body. He then got a skull saw. The street phrase "peel your cap" obviously came from this procedure.

After the DME cut into the skull, the skin from the base of the skull was pulled forward over the face. The top of the decedent's skull was removed, and the brain examined, weighed, and placed in a metal bowl for further examination. There was obvious head trauma as a result of at least one gunshot wound to the head. The DME located the bullet fragment that had lodged inside of Helford's skull. The projectile was subsequently cataloged and released to Hawley and I. This particular projectile was a critical piece of evidence. It would subsequently be taken to our Firearm Analysis Unit to be compared for type and caliber and entered into the National Integrated Ballistics Information Network (NIBIN) database to be compared to other firearms crimes.

The DME conducted what was known as a "Y" incision to examine the body for trauma and determine what organs were damaged by the gunshots. Helford's body was also being examined to gather serology evidence due to what appeared to be a violent sexual assault (rape).

The DME advised Hawley and me that Michelle's primary cause of death was due to multiple gunshot wounds (GSW) to her body as well as the single GSW she had sustained to the head. There was also evidence that she had been sexually assaulted due to vaginal trauma consistent with forcible rape. Hawley and I left the coroner's office and drove back to SBH to begin the search for the assholes responsible for her brutal rape/murder.

Possible Eyewitness

While organizing the murder book and reviewing witness statements, we noted there was a female that lived on 97th Street whose bedroom window faced the north/south alley. According to her statement, she had observed two male Hispanics and one male Black, who had a "CXL" tattoo on one side of his neck. They all ran out of the alley in a northeasterly direction immediately after several gunshots had been fired in that alley. So now we had a possible lead. Hawley immediately contacted the Detective Support Division-Gang Unit to procure a Cal-Gangs printout of the Carnales Street Gang, aka CXL, which meant, "Brothers."

The Carnales Street Gang's "territory" extended from Manchester Avenue on the south to Florence Avenue on the north, west to the Harbor Freeway and east to Main Street. So, we were investigating a Southeast Patrol Division murder that happened on the northern border of Manchester Avenue. The Carnales Street Gang is located within 77th Street Patrol Division.

Hawley and I conducted a follow up to confirm the possible eyewitness' statement. During the interview, we learned that her brother had been shot and killed by a Carnales gang member. In the meantime, Hawley had contacted the gang officers responsible for gathering intelligence on Carnales. Hawley was introduced to an associate CXL, a young man by the name of Griego, who had previously been an LAPD Explorer. Griego advised Hawley that Carnales had a couple of Black male gang members.

Investigative Travel

Within days, Hawley identified two possible suspects; one of whom resided in Kansas. There was information that he had a "CXL" tattoo on his neck. The most heinous crime anyone could commit against mankind is murder. The Los Angeles Police Department will pursue you to the ends of the Earth and pull out all the stops to apprehend you! Hawley made investigative travel arrangements for us to travel to Kansas. Our focus was to determine if the individual living in Kansas was one of our outstanding suspects. We flew to Kansas, met with the local Town Marshal, and determined our possible suspect was actually in Kansas on the day of Helford's murder. He was officially eliminated from our murder investigation.

Griego Killed In Gang-related Drive by Shooting

Sadly, while Hawley and I were in Kansas, Griego, the former LAPD Explorer, was shot and killed in an unrelated drive-by shooting in the area of 99th Street and Normandie Avenue. We also learned through our investigation that his uncle was an active Los Angeles Police Officer assigned to Harbor Patrol Division. The demise of Griego was totally unrelated, unexpected, and tragic.

Hawley and I continued to press forward with our murder investigation and learned that Griego's burial would take place at Green Hills Memorial Park, located at 27501 S. Western Avenue, Rancho Palos Verdes. This particular memorial park borders LAPD's Harbor Patrol Division, however, the Los Angeles County Sheriff's Department, Lomita Station, had law enforcement jurisdiction.

Green Hills Memorial Park Surveillance

We were still pursuing the Carnales murder suspects angle and had arranged for a photographer from our Scientific Investigation Division, Photo Section, to take photographs of those attending Griego's funeral. I recall sitting in a hot van at the interment site with Detective Talbot Terrell (RIP). Hawley had received military orders and reported for duty via the U.S. Army Reserves.

As Terrell and I sat in the van, we observed several gang members at Griego's funeral. We also noted his uncle, who was there to support his sister, Griego's mother. Terrell and I had checked out a department Ithaca 12-gauge shotgun and were adorned in our LAPD raid jackets.

We would only make ourselves known if it appeared that our brother officer Griego needed some type of assistance. We ended up contacting the Los Angeles County Sheriff's Department, who responded and conducted several vehicle stops of gangsters who appeared to be armed. We stood by to ensure Officer Griego and his sister remained safe.

I never made contact with Officer Griego or told him that we were present at the interment site conducting surveillance. The thin blue line runs long and deep! My thoughts, prayers, and condolences go out to the Griego family for their loss. We would eventually eliminate the Carnales street gang as suspects in the murder investigation of Helford.

Approximately one week later, while sitting at my desk, I received a telephone call from the aunt of one of Helford's best friends, a court reporter, she suggested that I should really look into "Shadow," aka Corey Dwight Lloyd, her niece's boyfriend. If you recall, this was the same individual who told Mendoza that the last time he saw Helford alive was the night before her murder at around 7 p.m., when he allegedly gave her a cigarette then went home.

I advised the aunt that our investigation was still active, and we were exploring all avenues. I told her that everything was on the table.

If detectives are not able to solve a homicide investigation within the first 60 days, they are required to complete an in-depth investigative report. I used to refer to it as, "penalty paper."

New Lead - (Former LAPD Explorer)

I received a telephone message from another former LAPD Explorer; Mr. Sosa who was now a real estate agent. Sosa disclosed that he had information on the Michelle Helford murder. I called Sosa, who divulged that he was in the process of assisting one of his clients, C Rodriguez, to list her home for sale at 120 West 98th Street, Los Angeles. According to Sosa, Rodriguez expressed him that her daughter, Mendoza, had information about a murder that had occurred and knew those who were responsible. Sosa further disclosed that the victim was a White female. This was a huge break; I wrote down Sosa's statement and immediately notified Lieutenant Robelto of the news. Hawley was still out on military leave, but would be returning within the week.

Follow Up and Happy Meal

Armed with new information, thanks to Mr. Sosa, I conducted a follow-up at 120 West 98th Street, Los Angeles. I door knocked the location and Mendoza answered the front door again. I had my game face on and did not hold back any punches. I advised Mendoza that I had just received credible information that she knew the suspects responsible for the brutal murder of Michelle Helford. I informed Mendoza that based on my information she could either be a cooperative witness or a suspect. Mendoza tearfully agreed to voluntarily ride with me to SBH to be formally interviewed.

If Mendoza had refused to be cooperative, unbeknownst to her, she would have been arrested and charged as an accessory or accomplice in the murder of Michelle Helford. Mendoza made the right decision. She looked at me and said, "Sir, I don't have a babysitter. Is it OK to bring my baby?" I replied, "Absolutely." I escorted Mendoza and her child to my police vehicle, advised Communications Division to show me en route from 120 West 98th Street to 4125 South

Crenshaw Boulevard with one female and provided my mileage. While en route, Mendoza disclosed to me that she did not have any money and her baby was hungry. I drove to McDonalds and purchased a Happy Meal for her son.

Critical Homicide Interview

The interview room was set up. I took Michelle Helford's Murder Book into the room and began my interview/interrogation of Mendoza. I explained to Mendoza that I was only interested in the truth and nothing but the truth. She broke down and provided a full statement.

According to Mendoza, "On the night Michelle was murdered, she was staying with me." Helford had run away from her foster parent's residence in Rancho Cucamonga to hang out in Los Angeles. Mendoza disclosed that Helford went outside and decided to walk across the street to Sugar Bear's residence, 117 West 98th Street. Mendoza said that she went with Helford and identified those present inside of the residence that evening as, Sugar Bear, Pirate, Shadow, and her brother, Chavo.

According to Mendoza, they were playing "Spin the Bottle," and everyone was stripped down to under garments. Mendoza shared that Chavo had lost and was directed by Sugar Bear to go into his bedroom to Jack off Pirate!" At that point, Mendoza said that she decided to leave, but recalled that Helford walked into the bedroom believing Chavo was going to actually "Jack off Pirate!"

Mendoza shared that Sugar Bear, Pirate, and Shadow told her they had killed Helford. According to Mendoza, on the night of Helford's murder, Sugar Bear, Pirate, and Shadow all walked with Helford westbound down 98th Street until they reached the north/south alley just east of Broadway before shooting her to death. When I asked Mendoza how she knew about that, she replied, "Sugar Bear, Pirate, Shadow, and Chavo all told her." According to Mendoza, during our initial interview, on the day of Helford's murder she was intimidated by the presence of Sugar Bear and Pirate, who were standing in the yard next door, and that's why she couldn't share what she knew. Mendoza further disclosed that Shadow was the Black male she had spoken to on the morning of Michelle's murder. Mendoza was shown several suspect photographic six-packs and given a photographic admonition. Mendoza positively identified all three suspects responsible for the brutal rape/murder of Michelle Helford.

Honorary Pallbearers

SHOCKING: Listed as honorary pallbearers on Helford's funeral program were suspects Corey Dwight Lloyd, aka Shadow, and Ramon Raul Lopez, aka Sugar Bear.

Hawley and I seized a photocopy of Helford's funeral obituary. Listed, as honorary pallbearers were suspects Corey Dwight Lloyd, aka Shadow, and Ramon Raul Lopez, aka Sugar Bear. So, not only did these suspects brutally rape and murder Helford, they attended her funeral and volunteered to be honorary pallbearers. It was obvious these assholes had no remorse and absolutely no conscience or soul.

Law and Order

Now, it was time to file murder charges and hunt down the suspects responsible for this brutal, senseless, and cowardly rape/murder. By this time, Hawley had returned from his military commitment. We conducted site surveys for search warrants of 117 West 98th Street, Los Angeles, where the brutal sexual assault/rape took place, residence of suspect Sugar Bear.

Early during the investigation, I had received information from the aunt of L. Gibson, who informed me that Shadow (Corey Lloyd) was currently living in the city of Rialto with Gibson. I contacted Rialto Police Department's Street Crime Attack Team (SCAT) and confirmed the residence located on Lilac Avenue north of Foothill Boulevard.

Search Warrant and Case Filed

Hawley completed the search warrant affidavit, and we conducted a follow up at the Los Angeles County District Attorney's Hardcore Gang Unit, Compton Superior Courthouse. We presented our case to the filing Deputy District Attorney (DDA). After the DDA reviewed our murder book and read the extensive follow-up reports. Multiple counts of murder, kidnapping, rape, firearm charges, and the gang enhancement for committing a felony for the benefit of a gang were filed against the suspects (Case No. TA 019920).

We procured felony arrest warrants for all three of our outstanding suspects. A Superior Court judge reviewed and signed the search warrant affidavit, which gave us the authority to search the suspect's residence for evidence of the crime and to procure DNA serology trace evidence from all three suspects for the rape allegation.

Tactical Operations Plan

Hawley put together our tactical operations plan for the search warrant service of 117 West 98th Street. After recruiting other detectives and uniformed officers, we would serve the search warrant during the early morning hours on the following day. However, since, Shadow (Corey Lloyd) lived in Rialto, I wanted to personally hook his ass up!

Arrest of Corey Dwight Lloyd in Rialto

"You're Corey Lloyd correct? My name is Maurice Landrum; I am a detective from the Los Angeles Police Department assigned to South Bureau Homicide. Well, Corey, I have good news and some bad news for you. The good news is we know who raped and murdered Michelle. The

bad news is, Corey, I have a felony arrest warrant issued in your name for the rape and murder of Michelle Helford!"

Finally, it was time to arrest these assholes for the brutal rape/murder of victim Michelle Helford. I drove to Rialto and met with Sergeant Pierson from Rialto Police Department. He was the officer in charge of SCAT, which was like my former SPU position at Southwest Patrol Division. In any event, he was briefed and received photographs of our outstanding suspects including, Corey Lloyd. We drove to Lloyd's last known address, and I made contact with his girlfriend Gibson. After identifying myself, I informed Gibson that Lloyd was wanted for the rape and murder of Helford, her best friend. Gibson looked at me, broke down, and started crying. She told me that Lloyd was up the street visiting some friends. Time was of the essence. I told Gibson to call Lloyd and tell him that the baby had gotten sick and she really needed him to come home to take her to Kaiser Permanente Urgent Care. Gibson made the call as I had requested. I listened in as she explained the urgency to Lloyd about the baby being sick and the need for him to come home to take them to the hospital in Fontana. I will never forget Lloyd's response.

He told Gibson, "Fuck you, bitch. Catch the bus!" When she hung up the phone, I asked Gibson if she knew where Lloyd's friend lived. According to Gibson, the friend lived a couple of blocks away. I remember thinking to myself, "We have guns and will travel. If Lloyd won't come to us, we will go to him!"

Gibson and her baby got into my police vehicle, and we began heading northbound on Lilac Avenue. When we approached the intersection of Lilac Avenue and Grove Street, Gibson pointed to Lloyd, who was driving his vehicle and had stopped for the stop sign at the intersection at Grove Street, facing southbound on Lilac Avenue. I immediately advised Sergeant Pierson, who directed his officers. They began to follow Lloyd, who drove into the parking lot of his apartment complex. This was the moment that I had been waiting for.

As members of the Rialto Police Department's SCAT tactically surrounded Lloyd's vehicle with MP-5 submachine guns deployed, I took the opportunity to walk up to re-introduce myself. This was my exact conversation with Lloyd: "You're Corey Lloyd, correct? My name is Maurice Landrum. I am a detective from the Los Angeles Police Department, assigned to South Bureau Homicide. Well, Corey, I have good news and some bad news for you. The good news is, we know who raped and murdered Michelle. The bad news is, Corey, I have a felony arrest warrant issued in your name for the rape and murder of Michelle Helford!"

Rialto SCAT ordered Lloyd out of his vehicle at gunpoint. I, personally, hooked him up with my pair of Peerless handcuffs and placed his sorry ass in the front seat of my police vehicle to be transported back to SBH. I informed Lloyd that he and I were going to get a chance to bond as I transported his punk ass back to SBH.

Lloyd and I had a heart-warming conversation about life. I warned him that if he tried any felony stupid shit, that I would have no problem shooting him multiple times. Needless to say, our drive was uneventful. While en route, I notified Hawley that Lloyd was in custody, and that we were en route to SBH. Upon our arrival, Lloyd was placed in the interview room to be interrogated and processed.

Search Warrant and Arrest

Now, it was time to take down, Ramon Raul "Sugar Bear" Lopez. It was time to make that early morning house call at 117 West 98th Street along with several SBH detectives and LAPD uniformed officers. Upon our arrival, Southeast officers tactically deployed around Lopez's residence, Knock-and-notice was given and entry was made into the residence. Lopez was taken into custody in his bedroom. He was asleep on the top bunk of his bunk bed, armed with a semi-automatic pistol.

Scientific Investigation Division (SID) processed the location and gathered DNA serology evidence. I recalled SID cutting away a large portion of carpet and seizing a mattress as evidence. While searching Lopez's closet, I observed a Rubbermaid trash can full of marijuana that had been drying out. I remember talking to his mother, who spoke broken English, and asking her if she was aware that her son had a trash can full of weed in his closet.

She responded, "Yes, he pulled those weeds in the backyard." I explained that I was not talking about yard weeds; I was talking about weed as in marijuana. After SID completed processing the crime scene, we cleared the location with Sugar Bear in custody and en route to SBH to be interviewed. Two in custody, one more to go!

Joel Guzman Cortez, aka "Pirate," Surrenders

A follow up was conducted at the last-known address (mother's residence) of Joel Guzman Cortez, aka Pirate. According to Cortez's mother, she had not heard from him in a couple of days. I advised her that Cortez was wanted for murder and needed to turn himself in to any local law enforcement agency. I told her that based on the crime, he was considered armed, dangerous, and officers would not hesitate to use whatever force necessary to apprehend him, including, but not limited to, the use of deadly force. I left her my business card and told her to call me, if she heard from him. I cleared the location and drove back to SBH. Cortez's mother convinced him to surrender to the Los Angeles County Sheriff's Department at Norwalk Station.

Interrogation Time

Cortez was eventually transported to SBH to be interrogated with the other two Adam Henrys! During the interrogations, I advised the trio separately of course that the search warrant granted us the authority to have medical personnel procure DNA serology evidence, such as pubic hairs, blood, urine, and buccal swabs, to analyze. Helford's serology report disclosed that she had contracted first-stage gonorrhea.

During the interrogation with Cortez, he stated, "Michelle wanted me, but I just sat on the couch that night because my girlfriend had burned me." When

I asked Cortez to clarify what he meant by "My girlfriend had burned me?" he replied, "My girlfriend gave me gonorrhea." Bingo! Cortez did two things for me to seal his faith. First, he placed himself at the scene of the rape/murder and secondly, he had gonorrhea.

Criminal Justice System

There are four punishment philosophies when it comes to incarceration. They are identified as deterrence, incapacitation, rehabilitation, and retribution. Of these philosophies, in terms of the crime these assholes committed, retribution was the goal. They had committed the ultimate crime: raping and shooting to death a 15-year-old female. They showed no remorse, no emotion, no regret. When you look at the punishment options, it is clear what this trio deserved: Life in prison without the possibility of parole or the death penalty:

- **Deterrence** - The sole purpose of this punishment philosophy is to prevent crime from being committed, convincing others that punishment will be handed down for violating the law.
- **Incapacitation** - Incapacitation involves attempts to physically restrain offenders from victimizing others.
- **Rehabilitation** - Rehabilitation is used to change or correct an offender's criminal behavior. Rehabilitation is a form of specific treatment offered to criminals while in or out of custody to reduce the fear and incidence of criminal behavior.
- **Retribution** - In the modern era, retribution is referred to as "just desserts" justice. In other words, harsh punishment to fit the crime. For example, an offender that murders someone under the theory of retribution is expected to receive life in prison without the possibility of parole or the death penalty.

Court Trial, Pasadena Superior Court

Normally, a murder that took place in Southeast Patrol Division was filed and tried at the Compton Superior Court. However, that court was so impacted that the only open courtroom was located at the Pasadena Superior Courthouse. This case had been filed with the Los Angeles County District Attorney Hardcore Gangs Unit and would be transferred and tried in Pasadena. Before we reached this point, Lopez, at 17 years old, had been declared unfit and unable to be rehabilitated in the juvenile court system. A fitness hearing was heard in the Compton Juvenile Court, and Lopez was ruled unfit and certified to be tried as an adult. Game on now!

Court Case No. TA 019920

The jury was selected and sworn in, and opening statements commenced. I was assigned as the Case Investigating Officer (Case I/O). It was time to give Helford a voice and seek justice for her and for those who loved her. The prosecutor presented his case-in-chief, which established a motive for Helford's brutal murder: a cover up for the gang rape. The jury heard from several critical witnesses, including the Deputy Medical Examiner, who had performed the autopsy. As the I/O, I was called upon as a witness to testify about my investigation and how the defendants were identified and taken into custody. During direct examination, one of the defendants' attorneys wanted to discuss an issue with the judge, who called a side-bar discussion that was conducted in the presence of the jury, defendants, and me.

I recalled Lopez looking up and giving me the middle finger while mouthing, "Fuck you!" What a special moment. I wished there was a legal way for me to walk up to him in the presence of the jury and just slap the fudge out of his ass. In any event, I looked at the jury and the little old lady from Pasadena, seated in the front row made eye contact and appeared to nod as if to say, "Don't worry about that asshole." The sidebar issue involved jury instructions, which the judge resolved. After my testimony, the prosecutor released me, but had me placed on-call. The work of a homicide investigator never stops; I was in the middle of another unrelated homicide investigation during that time.

Jury Deliberation

Final arguments and jury instructions were completed, and the jury now had a chance to digest the brutal rape and murder of Michelle Helford and deliver justice. The jury deliberated less than a full day before returning with verdicts. Please keep in mind that because of the age of Lopez (17) during the commission of the crime, the death penalty was not an option. Had he been an adult at the time of this heinous crime, the death penalty would have been strongly considered.

Guilty Verdicts

I get a call from the prosecutor that the jury had reached verdicts, which would be read after lunch. I drove out to the Pasadena Superior Courthouse and sat quietly as the courtroom clerk reviewed the verdicts submitted by the jurors. She handed the verdict forms to the judge, who read the verdicts into the record. Well, it was time for these assholes to learn their well-deserved punishment. They were all found **GULITY** of conspiracy to commit murder, which is the same as being convicted of first-degree murder. Finally, justice for Helford!

I stood by holding the courtroom door for the jurors, as they filed out of the courtroom one-by-one ending their jury service. There were several female jurors, who were in tears as they walked out. I thanked them all for their service and waited as everyone had cleared the courtroom except the defendants and the court bailiffs. Lopez looked back at me, so I took the opportunity to return the favor. I grabbed the bottom of my tie held it up and saluted him with my middle finger, and mouthed to him, "You are a convicted rape murdering asshole. Enjoy that prison life." I am retired now and these assholes are still in prison. Lloyd and Cortez were sentenced to life without the possibility of parole, aka LWOP. Lopez was sentenced to 25 years to life, Case No. TA 019920.

Defendants: Public Information

Corey Dwight Lloyd, aka **Shadow** CDCR No. H94391; California State Prison, L.A. County

Joel Guzman Cortez, aka **Pirate** CDCR No. H93685; Avenal State Prison

Ramon Raul Lopez, aka **Sugar Bear** CDCR No. J05379; Chuckawalla Valley State Prison

CHAPTER 19

Michael Hubert Hughes (Serial Killer)

On Wednesday, September 23, 1992, I was assigned to South Bureau Homicide. My partner was on vacation, so Lieutenant Robelto had me team up with Detective II Carlos Brizzolara. We received a homicide call to Jesse Owens Park, located at 9651 South Western Avenue, Los Angeles, within 77th Street Patrol Division's jurisdiction, for a deceased Black female adult, who was partially nude.

Upon our arrival, 77th Street patrol officers had established a crime scene. Brizzolara and I signed the crime scene log and were escorted to a secluded area within the park. I recall walking along the side of a small dirt path surrounded by shrubbery. The decedent was lying in a supine position with both legs apart, partially nude from the waist down. Rigor mortis had set in, which meant the victim's joints and muscles had stiffened up.

That told me the decedent had been dead for close to eight hours. This was obviously some type of sexual assault, there was semen present in the vaginal area of the decedent, and ants were crawling around the decedent's neck and vaginal cavity. It appeared that the victim had defecated on herself. Based on the preliminary examination of the decedent's body, I decided that she must have been strangled. There was paperwork located near the decedent's body with the name of Michael Hughes on it. Although, it was early in our investigation, I felt Hughes was definitely a person of interest.

We began to process the crime scene, and other SBH detectives assisted us by interviewing people in the park. Based on those interviews, we were able to identify the decedent as Teresa M. Ballard; a 26-year-old female who based on interviews of witness disclosed that sadly she had an addiction to rock cocaine. Regardless of her drug addition, she was still someone's loved one and a victim of vicarious murder. The Los Angeles County Coroner Investigator responded to our location to conduct his on-scene preliminary investigation. He could not definitively give us an official cause of death, but thought she may have been strangled. We collected the evidence at the scene, which included the information on Michael Hughes. Carlos was the primary investigator on this case.

Autopsy

I attended the autopsy of Teresa Ballard with Brizzolara. The Deputy Medical Examiner collected DNA serology evidence, but he was unable to provide us with an official cause of death. We were advised that further forensic testing would have to be conducted. After several weeks, Brizzolara was advised by the Los Angeles County Coroner's Office that Ballard's official cause of death was strangulation, and her death was classified as a homicide. Brizzolara continued to work this case and pursue leads. He had disseminated wanted bulletins regarding Michael Hughes as a person of interest in the murder of Ballard.

Serial Killer: Michael Hughes

Back then, DNA technology was fairly new and LAPD did not have the resources at that time to have a DNA profile compared with other state, federal, and local law enforcement labs. It turned out that Michael Hughes was a serial killer, and our victim, Teresa Ballard, was actually his fifth homicide victim. All of his victims had been sexually assaulted late at night and strangled. Listed below are the homicide victims positively linked to serial killer Michael Hubert Hughes:

Victim's Name	Age	Date of Homicide
Yvonne Coleman	15	January 22, 1986
Verna Williams	36	May 26, 1986
Deborah Jackson	30	December 1, 1987
Deanna Wilson	30	August 30, 1990
Teresa M. Ballard	27	September 23, 1992
Brenda A. Bradley	37	October 5, 1992
Terri Myles	33	November 8, 1993
Jamie Harrington	29	November 14, 1993

Suspect Hughes was linked to the killing of three women on separate occasions, and he had dumped their bodies in alleys within an industrial area of Culver City. It was during the arrest for these murders that Hughes was linked to the death of Ballard via DNA. In 1998, Hughes was convicted of the deaths of four victims, including Ballard. He was sentenced to life without the possibility of parole. My thoughts, condolences, and prayers go out to all of the victims listed above.

Death Penalty

In September 2011, Los Angeles County Deputy District Attorney, Prosecutor Beth Silverman, contacted me regarding defendant Michael Hubert Hughes. According to Prosecutor Silverman, Hughes had been linked to three additional murders based on a cold hit DNA link and had been criminally charged for those murders. The trial was scheduled to begin in October 2011, and I was subpoenaed to testify for what was known as California Evidence Code §1101(b), information to provide testimony about Hughes' pattern of conduct as it related to the sexual assault and strangulation murder of Ballard.

Court Case No. BA332099

On Tuesday, November 1, 2011, I appeared in Department 103 at 210 West Temple Street and testified in the murder case against convicted murder Michael Hughes. I gave direct testimony and was briefly cross-examined by Hughes' defense attorney. The jury returned a verdict of guilty in the first degree and deliberated about whether or not Hughes should be sentenced to death. He had already been sentenced to life without the possibility of parole for the murder of Ballard and the three other victims' rape/murders.

Thanks to the tenacious investigative efforts of Los Angeles Police Department's Robbery Homicide Division Detectives Shepard and Coulter, who went over all the evidence from several cases linked to Hughes, including follow-ups to where Hughes was being housed in Kern County, it was confirmed that Hughes was responsible for the other rape murders.

Hughes was convicted and condemned to death for his murderous crime spree. I would like to also thank, Prosecutor Beth Silverman for presenting the facts and advocating for the victims and their families. His conviction will not bring back the victims, but justice will be served!

Defendant: Public Information

(Death Row)

CDC# P25039 Date: 07/02/2012

| Michael Hubert Hughes | CDCR No. P25039 | **Condemned** | San Quentin State Prison |

CHAPTER 20

Northeast Community Patrol Station

Promoted to Sergeant

O n June 12, 1994, I was promoted to the rank of Sergeant I and assigned to Northeast Patrol Division. I remember this date well because when the promotion transfer list was released, I was vacationing on the beaches in Waikiki, Hawaii. Well, it was time for a new challenge. "Patrol Ready," now I would be assuming my new role of leading the fine men and women of the Los Angeles Police Department and providing my patrol and investigative expertise. I had some great homicide partners who also had dual status. One of my co-workers, Detective II Lou Leiker, asked me to schedule the two-week supervisory school as soon as possible. According to Leiker, supervisors aren't official until they complete the mandatory California peace officers supervisor's training course.

I knew I was on the list to be promoted after the Rodney King incident. Numerous newly promoted supervisors, especially majorities, were being transferred to Valley Bureau. Believing that I would be one of those casualties, my wife and I decided to move. We rented a three-bedroom apartment at 3701 Overland Avenue, J294 in Los Angeles. Obviously, my thinking was to avoid the freeway therapy. We had moved the entire day before, and I was scheduled to work my first shift as a new sergeant on Morning Watch.

I was tired, so I contacted my new Lieutenant Mark Perez to see if I could take the day off. According to Lt. Perez, he needed me to come in. So, I sucked it up and went to work. During my first night, I attended roll call and sat quietly as Lt. Perez introduced me. One thing you learn quickly is that Los Angeles Police Officers have a network. They will contact friends and associates where you were previously assigned to gather intelligence about you. I knew I was the genuine article in terms of working patrol and detectives. I actually earned my promotion through hard work, not being sponsored or nepotism.

I didn't have a sponsor like many of the past and present command staff. I can say without a shadow of a doubt that one of the biggest reasons I didn't have a sponsor was I refused to kiss the ring. So, I was not part of the nepotism and cronyism that was prevalent throughout LAPD. In any event, some folks wanted to test my knowledge as it related to department policy and patrol operations.

Back then, Volume Four, Section 700 was where you would look for answers to the majority of patrol-related policies and procedures. Common sense was not in the department manual; you either had it or you didn't! One important thing I picked up was that every policy had a section titled "Supervisor's Responsibilities." I made sure I knew what my responsibilities were for any field situation as a field supervisor.

Northeast Patrol Division, aka Northeast Community Police Station, provided police services to the communities of Atwater Village, Cypress Park, Eagle Rock, East Hollywood, Echo Park, Elysian Park Valley, Glassell Park, Griffith Park, Highland Park, Los Feliz, Mt. Washington, and Silverlake. Northeast was approximately 29 square miles with a population of approximately 250,000 people.

Northeast Area Reporting District Map

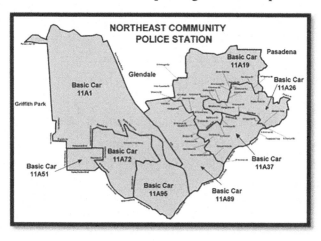

Vehicle and Foot Pursuit

It is my first night as a Sergeant of Police; I was teamed up with Sergeant Robles, a seasoned veteran. While driving around, a morning watch patrol unit advised Communications Division that they were in pursuit of a stolen vehicle heading toward Avenue 30 and Carlyle Street in the Glassell Park area of the division. The air unit was now overhead and the "night sun" (its spotlight) shone down on the suspect's vehicle. Robles and I were headed to the general area. While en route, Robles told me how this was a baby vehicle pursuit and that it should be an easy one for me to investigate and complete.

The joys of being the junior sergeant! As the new sergeant, you are guaranteed to be assigned any vehicle pursuits, use-of-force investigations and an occasional personnel complaint investigation. Meanwhile, the air unit's night sun had gotten closer and closer to our location. I could hear sirens blaring louder and louder. Suddenly the primary pursuing unit broadcast that they were in foot pursuit of the suspects, who had bailed out of the stolen vehicle. Now it's game time. You have to take several things into consideration when in foot pursuit. Besides being wanted for the obvious, a stolen vehicle, what other crimes might the suspects be wanted for? Are the suspects' armed? These are important factors to determine what tactics will be employed to safely apprehend the suspects.

It's like an episode of *Cops,* except there are no cameras. The only audience is the suspects and police officers. By this time, both suspects had run to within several feet of Robles and me. They continued running between the houses, as they were pursued on-foot by two sergeants and two officers. Robles and I exited our police vehicle and joined the foot pursuit. I was fired up to see working sergeants. That was not the norm for sergeants to be in foot pursuit. Officers, who had monitored the foot pursuit, had deployed on the next block. The suspects ran out of real estate and were taken into custody without incident. I remember interviewing the driver of the primary unit that was in pursuit, Police Officer II Carolyn Allen and her partner.

Robles dropped me off at the station to complete the Vehicle Pursuit Report. I had the ACC operator at the station print out a copy of the entire incident, which helped me reconstruct the pursuit route and vehicle violations committed by the suspect. I believe Robles may have thought that it was going to take me half of the watch to complete the pursuit report. I was done in approximately one hour; the vehicle pursuit forms were straightforward. Plus, I had an excellent pursuit report exemplar to follow.

One of the pursuing officers, Officer Trujillo, while in foot pursuit, had severely sprung his ankle and was unable to safely operate his personal vehicle, a standard-shift pickup truck. Once again, being the lowest supervisor on the totem pole, I was delegated to drive him home, which was located in San Bernardino County past the Cajon Pass. Officer Trujillo had his partner, Officer Tejon, drive home his personal vehicle. Needless to say, I was hurting for certain. Mission accomplished, Officer Tejon and I drove back to Northeast Station and went end-of-watch. Night one done and in the books!

Day two

Well, it was another wonderful day in the neighborhood. I was present as Lieutenant Perez conducted roll call. I learned that Sergeant Robles had gone out on injured on-duty (IOD) status, as a result of our prior foot pursuit. Robles, who was near retirement, did not return to duty during the remainder of my time at Northeast Patrol Division.

For my second night, I was teamed up with Sergeant Jerry O'Neil, a former air support pilot. O'Neil was a wealth of knowledge; he drove me around the entire Division and showed me several driving short cuts. For example, York Boulevard and Colorado Boulevard were the quickest thoroughfares to get to North Figueroa Street. Hyperion Boulevard was the quickest short cut to what we called the Hollywood side of the Division. I remembered being driven out to Zoo Drive, located in Griffith Park off the Interstate 5 freeway. As we drove in the secluded area, there were several single, male motorists hanging out involved in vice activity.

Homicide off Zoo Drive

Approximately, two weeks later, Northeast patrol units received a radio call of a man down near the soccer fields off of Zoo Drive. I was familiar with the area thanks to Jerry. Upon my arrival, I observed a male Hispanic wearing black pants, a white collared dress shirt, and cowboy boots. He was lying in a supine position (on his back) with what appeared to be a single gunshot wound in his chest. Los Angeles City Fire Paramedics were on scene and pronounced the unidentified victim dead or DRT. I directed officers to cordon off the area, start a crime scene log and look for evidence. Proper notifications were made, and homicide detectives were en route to the scene.

The decedent appeared to have been in his early forties. I recalled thinking it was probably a drug deal gone wrong. I spoke to Detective III Jim McCann, Northeast Homicide Detective Coordinator, and told him I wouldn't be surprised if the decedent had an envelope taped to his chest full of money. The Los Angeles County Coroner's Investigator arrived and began the on-scene investigation. In order to examine the decedent's gunshot wound to the upper torso, the Coroner Investigator unbuttoned the decedent's shirt and found, taped to the decedent's stomach, an envelope that contained U.S. currency. I completed my first-responder's supervisor statement and cleared the scene after the coroner removed the body.

After three months on Morning Watch, I was rotated to PM Watch. Lieutenant Byron Young was the PM Watch Commander and Sergeant II Joe Hermann was the Assistant Watch Commander. I had a great time on Mid-PM watch. The Mid PM watch officers were go-getters. During roll call training, I would facilitate the department's standardized roll call training in addition to what I called "interactive scenarios." I would write up a caper and have the senior officers and probationary officers discuss how they would handle the call and what resources they would request. My primary goal was to enhance the thinking and officer safety of those officers.

Those interactive scenarios made my job as a field supervisor easier. For instance, I would respond to a crime scene and officers would have already taken the initiative to start a crime scene log, canvass the area for witnesses and evidence, and cordon off the crime scene.

During the winter months, Northeast Patrol Division because of its geographical location, would sometimes be bone-chilling cold. I was all about officer safety and often would tell my officers during roll call to use caution when conducting investigative stops of suspects wearing zarapes because they could conceal a sawed-off shotgun.

Well, one night, Narcotics Division was conducting an investigation in an apartment complex off of Edgemont Street on the Hollywood side of the Division when, suddenly, Communications Division broadcast that narcotics officers were requesting help: "Shot's fired. Male armed with sawed-off shotgun wearing a zarape." We responded to the location and the suspect was taken into custody without incident.

Approximately six months after arriving at Northeast Patrol Division, Lieutenant Sergio Robelto, Officer-in-Charge of South Bureau Homicide, had contacted me about working a joint LAPD-FBI homicide detail called the Cooperative Murder Investigation Team (COMIT). Well, if you know me by now, then you know I couldn't pass up an opportunity to investigate and pursue some of Los Angeles's Most Wanted!

CHAPTER 21

South Bureau Homicide-COMIT

O
n December 25, 1994, Christmas Day, I was transferred back into South
Bureau Homicide to work as a member of the newly formed Cooperative
Murder Investigation Team (COMIT). Members of this joint Los Angeles
Police Department and Federal Bureau of Investigation detail were required to
submit their personal information for a federal background check to be cleared
to monitor a federal wire. After passing the background check, I was sworn-in
as a federal deputized marshal in order to monitor a federal wire. COMIT was
set up to perform three tasks:

1. Monitor a federal wire involving a notorious gang member
2. Review cold case murders
3. Conduct crimes against police officers, particularly officers being
    assaulted investigations

My partner during this time was Detective Trainee Chris Barling, who subsequently retired honorably as Detective III Chris Barling, 77th Division/Homicide Coordinator. During our review of one cold case murder, we focused on the murder of a gang member that had occurred in 1985 at the Chevron gas station located at 256 East Manchester Avenue, Los Angeles. According to the original homicide investigator, a person of interest in the murder had been identified as I.B. Lucky. However, the sole witness in the case was never interviewed. The 1985 homicide was a gang-related murder, and the sole witness was a gang member. It has been my experience that getting a gang member to come forward to provide information, a statement, or to testify in court was rare, if not impossible.

During my review of the 1995 South Bureau Homicide Victim's Log, I noted there was a homicide victim identified as, I.B. Lucky. He was shot and killed in the area of Van Ness Avenue between 54th Street and Slauson Avenue. I wondered if he was the same I.B. Lucky listed as a person of interest in the 1985 cold case murder that we were reviewing.

Upon closer review, I.B. Lucky's photograph and physical description matched the description of the outstanding suspect listed from the 1985 cold case murder. Through department resources, I located the sole witness, who was serving time at the Federal Correctional Complex in Florence, Colorado, on an unrelated narcotics violation. Detective Barling and I procured investigative travel authority and conducted a follow up there.

Case "Cleared Other"

Detective Barling and I interviewed the witness. We read him the photographic admonition before we showed him what is commonly referred to as a photo six-pack of photographs. (A photograph line-up consists of six individual photographs, one of which is your suspect). Upon reviewing them, he positively identified I.B. Lucky as the suspect that had shot and killed his homeboy.

At that point, I directed the witness to circle his selection as well as write his initials and the date. Just like that, Barling and I solved the 1985 gang-related cold case murder. In this case, the suspect responsible was deceased. I completed the follow-up report to close out this particular cold case murder as, "cleared other." Since I.B. Lucky was deceased, "cleared other" was the appropriate crime disposition. Barling and I felt lucky to close out that particular cold case murder!

Ambush of LAPD Officers

Get ready to hear about an ambush of two Southeast patrol officers in the Jordan Downs Housing Development, Watts. Late one evening, Southeast Patrol Officers were involved in a vehicle pursuit that terminated in the Jordan Downs Housing Development. Several police units had responded and begun helping the primary unit establish a perimeter for the outstanding suspects, who had foot bailed. When Officer Josie Agnew and her partner arrived on scene, a suspect fired upon them. In fact, one of the rounds narrowly missed striking Officer Agnew in the head and had lodged in her sun visor just above her head on the driver's side of their police vehicle. Officers requested help and immediately set up a large perimeter, locking down the area. Numerous resources flooded the area, LAPD officers from surrounding patrol divisions, two air units, and Metropolitan K-9 units.

During a canvass of the immediate area, several eyewitnesses were located seated inside a parked vehicle in the parking lot, just feet away from where the suspect had fired his weapon at Officer Agnew. Based on the nature of this incident, the attempted murder of a Los Angeles Police Officer, my partner and I were called out to the scene to conduct our criminal investigation.

During the on-scene investigation, evidence was located, photographed, and booked. My partner and I went to Southeast Station to interview an eyewitness to the shooting. During the interview, we learned the suspect's gang moniker and got a description of what he had been wearing, a yellow Ducks' hockey jersey. Also, based on expended casings located, photographed, and collected as evidence, we were looking for a .45 caliber Glock semi-automatic pistol.

Suspect Identified, Search Warrant Procured

Timing is everything. Based on the outstanding suspect's gang moniker, he was positively identified and his last-known address was determined to be in the Jordan Downs Housing Development. A search warrant was written for the sole purpose of searching the suspect's residence for the outstanding firearm, clothing, and anything that would link him to the attempted murder of Los Angeles Police Officer Josie Agnew. Based on the totality of the circumstances, our search warrant was endorsed for nighttime service.

The investigation was approximately five hours old when we deployed on the search warrant location with uniformed officers as the entry team. Knock and notice was given, and uniformed officers entered the location followed by my partner and I.

The suspect was located in his bedroom, still wearing the yellow Ducks hockey jersey. A Glock .45 caliber semi-automatic pistol was located underneath his mattress, photographed, and seized. The suspect was transported to Southeast Station, interrogated, and booked for the attempted murder of LAPD Police Officer II Josie Agnew. During the interrogation, the suspect bragged about being a part of a crew that transported narcotics from Louisiana to California via Greyhound bus. That information was forwarded to Narcotics Division.

Type and Caliber Comparison

The firearm seized during the search warrant and the expended casings located and seized on the night of the attempted murder were checked out of evidence, and transported to the Firearm Analysis Unit (FAU), where a type-and-caliber examination and comparison were conducted to determine if the firearm seized was the same firearm used in the attempted murder of Officer Agnew. FAU conducted their examination and comparison, which determined the firearm seized was the same firearm used in the crime.

Criminal Charges Filed

The Los Angeles County District Attorney Office has a special prosecution unit that specifically prosecutes crimes against police officers, known as CAPOS. This particular case was presented to the Deputy District Attorney Filing Prosecutor, who filed numerous felony charges against the suspect. He was subsequently convicted and sentenced to 25 years to life. In your LAPD coloring book, you could color his ass gone!

Harbor Patrol Division

(Patrol Sergeant)

On October 1, 1995, I requested to be loaned out to Harbor Patrol Division as a Field Sergeant. My wife, a Los Angeles County Deputy Sheriff, had just been assigned to work Carson Station. Obviously, I wanted to be somewhat close in the event, she became involved in a volatile situation. I worked Harbor Patrol Division for approximately one deployment period. According to Position Control Section, Harbor Patrol Division was over T/O, which meant they did not have an open position to justify my position as a field patrol supervisor. However, Southeast Patrol Division had a field supervisor opening. They were one patrol division north of Harbor Patrol Division and still within driving time to the city of Carson.

CHAPTER 22
Patrolling Watts

Southeast Area Reporting District Map

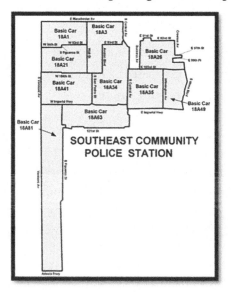

O n Sunday, November 26, 1995, I was transferred into Southeast Patrol Division as a Field Patrol Supervisor from Harbor Patrol Division. Southeast Community Police Station provided police services to the neighborhoods of Jordan Downs, Nickerson Gardens, Athens Park, San Miguel, Harbor Gateway, and Watts. There were approximately 150,000 residents within 10.2 square miles. Although only 10.2 miles, during the late 1990s, PCP, cocaine, and marijuana were prevalent. In addition, there was a major street gang problem that impacted the area as well. In fact, Southeast Division had 28 police officers, as well as, two Los Angeles County Probation Officers assigned to the Southeast CRASH Gang Unit.

I was assigned to PM Watch, which was extremely busy in terms of calls for service. Normally, supervisors are not assigned to handle radio calls for service. However, in Watts there were times we were assigned calls for service, including shootings-in-progress. During one shooting-in-progress, I was assigned to the suspect's vehicle was described as a gray Honda last seen heading westbound on 92nd Street from Maie Avenue. While en route eastbound on 92nd Street, from Central Avenue, I observed a gray Hyundai driving westbound at a high rate of speed from the shooting area.

I advised Communications Division of my observations, requested additional units as well as an air unit, negotiated a U-turn, and broadcasted that I was in vehicle pursuit of possible shooting suspects.

The suspect's vehicle turned southbound onto Pace Avenue from 92nd Street. While doing so, the front seat passenger tossed a revolver out of their window. I advised Communications Division to have a unit respond to the location and secure the weapon. Numerous patrol units joined me, so I relinquished my position in the pursuit to become the monitoring supervisor. The suspects eventually pulled over near 98th Street west of Central Avenue.

The primary and secondary units initiated a felony vehicle stop and ordered the suspects out of the vehicle. In a bizarre twist, witnesses from the original shooting scene had responded to our location, only to mad dog the suspects that were being taken into custody. The eyewitnesses—all gangsters, of course—refused to positively identify the suspects. Divisional detectives were notified, and they responded and took over the shooting investigation. Sadly, I lost count of the number of crime scenes I had responded to in Watts as a patrol supervisor. It was not uncommon to respond to several shooting crime scenes during a single work shift. There were a lot of guns on the streets of Watts, and the gangsters were not afraid to use them against their rivals or the police.

On March 2, 1996, South Bureau Homicide commended me for my involvement in the arrests of three suspects involved in a gang-related homicide that had occurred in Watts.

In August 1996, I sat in as the acting Southeast Watch Commander when Captain Mike Hillman, the Department's assigned On-Duty Command Duty Officer (CDO) walked into the watch commander's office. When I think of organizational leadership, Captain Hillman's name pops up. He was well respected and a proven leader. I recalled Captain Hillman asking me how was it going. I replied, "Sir, it would be going better if I was working for you!" Captain Hillman responded by telling me to fill out a request for transfer and/or change in paygrade (Form 1.40), and he would sign it.

I immediately filled out the form; Captain Hillman signed it before leaving Southeast Patrol Division that night. The Commanding Officer of Southeast Patrol, Captain Paul Pesqueira signed Form 1.40 the next day. I personally hand delivered it to Position Control Section downtown at the Parker Administration Building (PAB) aka Los Angeles Police Department's Headquarters, 150 N. Los Angeles Street, Los Angeles.

CHAPTER 23

Northeast Patrol, Second Tour

O n Sunday, September 1, 1996, I was transferred into Northeast Patrol Division as a Field Patrol Supervisor assigned to PM Watch. I was ecstatic; Captain Hillman had handpicked his supervisors. The majority of them were formerly assigned to Metropolitan Division: Sal Apodaca, Marty Koon, Ernie Haleck, John Del Vecchio, Kevin McClure, and Carlos De la Roca. Morale was extremely high, and the officers assigned to Northeast were motivated. During that time, Northeast Patrol Division was definitely a good place to work as a field supervisor and police officer.

All good things come to an end. Within two months of being transferred into Northeast, Captain Hillman was transferred to 77th Street Division. We were all ready to follow him when he advised us that Captain III Harlan Ward was the Area Commanding Officer and that he, Hillman, did not have control of the ship, so to speak! In the meantime, Captain Hale transferred into Northeast Division as the Patrol Commanding Officer as Captain Hillman's replacement. Lieutenant Lita Abella transferred into the Northeast Division as well.

SWAT Call Out

On November 16, 1996, I was sitting in as the acting PM Watch Commander. Officer Zarate and his partner, Officer Navarro, had responded to an unknown trouble call in the 3700 block of Los Feliz Boulevard. Upon their arrival, they spoke to Dr. Barlow, who had called about his son, Norman Barlow, who was drunk. Officer Zarate called me and wanted to know if they could book Norman for California Penal Code §647(f)-Drunk-in-Public because Dr. Barlow was concerned about his son's bizarre behavior. I remember saying, "You cannot arrest someone for being drunk inside of their own house! Are you kidding me?" I asked Officer Zarate if any crime had been committed; he replied, "No sir." I remember asking Officer Zarate to determine if Norman had access to any firearms within the residence. According to Officer Zarate, Dr. Barlow said he (himself) did own a firearm, but Norman did not have access to it. Officers Zarate and Navarro cleared the scene.

Norman the Barricaded Suspect

Approximately 20 minutes later, Police Officer III Roy Cook (RIP), assigned that night to the Northeast Division front desk, was talking with Dr. Barlow, who had walked into the lobby of the station. I overheard Dr. Barlow tell Officer Cook that his son, Norman, had gained control of his firearm within their residence and fired at least one round through the wall of the living. So, I walked up to the front desk to gather additional information. While Dr. Barlow was in the process of signing a crime report, I requested two additional units to meet me in the Watch Commander's office, Code 2. Based on his father's statement and the signed crime report, Norman had fired a gunshot inside an inhabited dwelling. We were also concerned about Norman's welfare. Dr. Barlow felt Norman might want to harm himself. He gave us the key to his residence so we could make entry to conduct the welfare check, seize the firearm, and arrest Norman. I also had Dr. Barlow draw us a diagram of the inside layout of his residence.

Officers Zarate, Navarro, Police Officer III Shameless and his probationary officer responded to the station. I briefed them and had Sergeant W meet us at the Los Feliz Boulevard location. During my tactical briefing, I looked the officers in the eyes and wanted to know if anyone had a problem with entering the location to conduct a welfare check on Norman. I also ensured that everyone was tacked up wearing ballistic vests and helmets. We went over the tactical plan, as well as, other tactical options. Sergeant W and a Police Officer I were deployed to the rear of the apartment complex in the event Norman decided to bail out of the rear window.

Neighbor Evacuated

Prior to making contact with Norman, we door knocked the neighbor's residence directly across the hall and informed the resident of our purpose. He advised us that the floor plan in Dr. Barlow's apartment was set up exactly like his apartment. We noted that the front door opened from left to right and that there was a living room to the left, kitchen/dining room area to the immediate right, long hallway straight ahead leading to a bedroom on the left, bathroom on the right, as well as, another bedroom around the corner.

Welfare Check

We had an obligation to conduct a welfare check. Norman's father had driven to the station to report his son had gained access to his firearm and fired at least one round inside of their apartment. He was concerned about Norman's mental stability. The entry team consisted of Officer Navarro, armed with the 870-department shotgun, Police Officer III Shameless, Police Officer II Zarate and me as the fourth entry team member. Police Officer I, and Sergeant W were covering the rear of the building as mentioned earlier.

Prior to entering the location, we attempted to establish contact via landline to Norman's telephone. There was no answer. So, we lined up and knocked on the door to announce our presence. There was still no answer. Based on the situation and the information we had, we needed to make entry into the location to see if Norman was inside and in need of medical assistance. Officer Shameless used the key to unlock the front door, and we made entry into the location while simultaneously announcing our presence. Still there was no answer. It was evident that at least one gunshot had been fired inside of the residence; there was a gunshot hole in the living room wall, which came from the bedroom. The floor plan was the same as the neighbor's: upon entering through the front door, the living room was to the left, dining area and kitchen were to the right, long narrow hallway straight ahead. Norman's bedroom was down the hall located on the left, a bathroom down the hall on the right and another bedroom was past the bathroom on the right.

Due to the tight quarters, I directed Navarro to sling the shotgun. Officer Shameless took the point as the designated contact officer followed by Officer Zarate and Navarro. I took up a position of advantage on the corner of the dining room and kitchen wall. Officer Shameless continued to make his way down the hallway. When he reached Norman's bedroom, he knocked and opened the door. That's when he came face-to-face with Norman, who was staring him down holding a loaded revolver underneath his own chin.

Barricaded Suspect

Officer Shameless immediately retreated, yelling, "He's got a gun, he's armed with a gun." Personally, I was pissed now! I hand signaled to the officers to find concealment, because, this was now a SWAT call out. I walked outside to make the proper notifications via cellphone to the station.

It was change-of-watch and Morning Watch had begun their shift. I contacted the Assistant Watch Commander, Sergeant II JJ to advise him that we were Code 6 on Los Feliz Boulevard and had a confirmed armed barricaded suspect. While talking to JJ over the phone, suddenly I hear, "Boom!"

I asked JJ to hang on for a second while I contacted Sergeant W via our hand-held radio to confirm whether a gunshot had been fired. Sergeant W confirmed it was a gunshot. I asked him if it was from our officers or the suspect. He replied, "Suspect." I updated JJ, who made the appropriate notifications, which included our commanding officers, Department Command Post, and, of course, Metropolitan Division (SWAT).

In the meantime, I requested additional units to assist with evacuating several residents in the direct line of fire for their safety and to reduce city liability. As SWAT arrived, I went to their command post and met with SWAT Commander, Lieutenant Thomas Runyen and Police Officer III+I Randal "Randy" Simmons (RIP) who was the designated crisis negotiator for this particular call-out. After being briefed, SWAT deployed their tactical plan and moved into position. Zarate, Navarro, Shameless, and the Police Officer I, were relieved of their positions by SWAT officers and redeployed on the outer perimeter. One of my former probationary officers, Wilson Wong and his partner Mike Gallegos took over the point at Norman's residence.

Simmons was able to establish communications with Norman and began to negotiate with him. Norman was kind of all over the place with his feelings. He kept saying that all he wanted was to be left alone and wanted everyone to go home. A couple of hours went by, and Simmons started to make significant progress. He advised Norman that no one wanted to hurt him. Norman was advised to put the gun down and walk out of his bedroom toward the front door. Norman reluctantly agreed and gave Simmons his word that he would exit his bedroom.

Exchange of Gunfire

Norman exited his bedroom. A large spotlight illuminated the entire hallway and living room area. There was one problem; Norman was still armed with the handgun. He raised his right arm, pointed the handgun in the direction of the spotlight, and discharged a round from his handgun.

Meanwhile, Wong and Gallegos, who were deployed near the front door, responded, an officer-involved shooting occurred. It sounded like someone playing the duck arcade shooting game, except this was real. Norman spun around after Wong and Gallegos returned fire at him and ran back into his bedroom yelling, "You guys lied!" Fortunately for him, he was not wounded during the exchange of gunfire. Meanwhile, the clinical psychologist on scene stated, "I think he really wants to give himself up."

I was in the field command post during this conversation when Lieutenant Runyen responded by saying, "Fudge that! Introduce gas into the location." Within minutes, Runyen's direct order was executed. Several canisters of tear gas were fired into the location. Approximately five minutes later, I heard what sounded like a shotgun round being fired. Next, SWAT officers notified the

Field Command Post that the suspect was in custody. I remember thinking Norman must be down! The next thing I hear via radio was a SWAT officer requesting a Northeast unit to take custody and control of Norman.

The Los Angeles Police Department's Elite Metropolitan Division SWAT Team once again de-escalated a potentially deadly situation. Norman was in custody. I remember walking to the black and white police vehicle where he was being held. I opened the rear back door and asked Norman why he didn't surrender peacefully. He replied, "I just want to be left alone." I replied, "Norman, you're a lucky man. When we initially entered your residence had I been the contact officer, we would not be having this conversation, you damn psycho!" It would not have been a SWAT call out. The only call out would have been our Robbery Homicide Division, Officer-Involved Shooting Team and the Los Angeles County Coroner's Office. I had to vent because our point officer, Officer Shameless, who himself had been armed, literally turned his back and retreated down the hallway yelling, "He's got a gun, he's armed with a gun!" I wasn't real happy with Officer Shameless, and he was about to hear about it during our tactical debriefing.

De-Briefing

We debriefed this tactical response, and I had no problem telling Officer Shameless that he compromised our entire entry team during the initial entry into the residence. Of course, he didn't want to accept it, so he went to a well-respected former SWAT Officer, Sergeant Ernie Haleck, who was assigned as a Sergeant at Northeast Patrol Station, and gave his version. When Haleck spoken to me and I gave him the real story, he concurred with me that Officer Shameless had compromised the team. I would work a couple more months on morning watch, before being transferred to PM watch, which was busier than morning watch. There was a lot of gang activity and narcotics being sold.

CHAPTER 24

Officer-Involved Shooting

(Fiddler on the roof)

O n Friday, February 21, 1997, I was assigned to Northeast Community Police Station working PM Watch as a Field Supervisor. During roll call in walks Detective Maria Foster, who was assigned to the Northeast Robbery Section. Detective Foster had fresh information about an outstanding suspect wanted for a robbery that had occurred at the K-Mart located at Fletcher and San Fernando Road. According to Detective Foster, there were two female suspects that had been arrested. We were provided with a description of the outstanding suspect, who she described as a male Hispanic adult with tattoos on both arms, a long ponytail down to his butt, possibly armed with a firearm. Detective Foster further disclosed that the suspect lived near Elita Place and Figueroa Street.

After roll call, I remained at the station to complete some administrative paper-work. In the meantime, the other sergeant working, John Del Vecchio had driven to Piper Tech to have his patrol car's converter comm (handheld radio transmitter) replaced. I completed my paperwork and cleared the station approximately 30 minutes later. I decided to drive to the area of Figueroa Street and Elita Place just to see if the suspect was in the area.

Suspect Located at Der Wienerschnitzel

I was in a black and white police vehicle in full uniform traveling northbound on Figueroa Street passing Avenue 52, approaching Elita Place. I looked over at the Der Wienerschnitzel located on the southwest corner of Figueroa Street at Elita Place and observed a male Hispanic adult with tattoos on both of his arms and a long ponytail. Now what are the chances of observing an individual hanging out who matches the description of the outstanding robbery suspect?

Well, I did what any good field supervisor was trained to do; I continued driving northbound on Figueroa Street to Avenue 54, where I made a U-turn while notifying Communications Division that I was requesting Northeast units and an air unit for a wanted 211 suspect loitering on the southwest corner of Figueroa Street at Elita Place. I provided a clothing description of the suspect as I began driving southbound on Figueroa Street towards Elita Place.

Unit 11A37 acknowledged my request and advised that they were 30 seconds out from my location. In the meantime, I was just north of the Der Wienerschnitzel, stopped in the number two lane of southbound traffic, tactically deployed behind the driver's door of the police vehicle, armed with my 92F Beretta semi-automatic pistol which I held in the low-ready position, focused in on the suspect. Suddenly, 11A37 was rolling Code 3, lights and siren on, traveling eastbound on Elita Place from Marimon Way toward Figueroa Street. The suspect suddenly looked in my direction, grabbed the fanny pack he was wearing around his waist, and took off running south towards Avenue 52 on Figueroa Street.

I advised Communications Division the suspect was now running south on Figueroa Street toward Avenue 52. Unit 11A37 simultaneously drove up and I yelled to them that the suspect was now heading westbound on Avenue 52. He had ran through the Arco gas station's parking lot, located on the northwest corner of Figueroa Street at Avenue 52. Believing the suspect was armed based on his furtive movements and seeing that he was near gas pumps, I made a quick decision to monitor his avenue of escape. Once the suspect ran through the gas station's parking lot, he ran northbound down the driveway of the first residence west of the gas station. At that point, I doubled back northbound and began to run westbound on Elita Place. I simultaneously updated Communications Division. Approximately two houses west of me, on the south side of Elita Place, the suspect began traversing fences still holding onto the fanny pack. I used whatever cover was available, including a couple of parked vehicles along the curb.

Fiddler on the Roof Shooting

I constantly updated Communications Division of my observations and the suspect's location. I was deployed behind a parked car located just east of 128 Elita Place when Police Officer III Mike Beloud and his probationer, Police Officer I Fernie Montesdeoca, drove up to my location. I had located the suspect standing on the pitched roof of 128 Elita Place. More importantly, I could clearly see the butt of a weapon in his right hand. The suspect began to turn in the direction of Officers Beloud and Montesdeoca, who were exiting their police vehicle. Based on the totality of the circumstances—suspect armed, officers in an exposed position—an officer-involved-shooting occurred.

From my position, the only clear shot I had was the suspect's lower extremity, specifically his right leg, so that's where I aimed. Upon being shot, the suspect immediately disappeared out of our view toward the other side of the pitched roof. I remember Beloud saying, "Hey Sarge, if you didn't shoot, I was about to." Communications Division was advised, "Shot's fired." Additional officers responded to the scene. I recalled being asked if we needed to set up a perimeter. I replied, "I know for a fact the suspect was struck by gunfire. I don't think, he is going to get too far on foot!" As the air unit flew overhead, they informed us that the suspect was on the roof bleeding profusely from his leg and smoking a cigarette with his hands up. The Los Angeles City Fire Department was summoned to assist with taking the suspect into custody. Officers John Hankins and Poochie were hoisted up via fire engine ladder; this was an awesome sight to see. Imagine two Los Angeles Police Officers, one armed with a shotgun and the other with his handgun going up on the roof. The LAPD air unit played a major role as the eyes from above. They directed the officers into position. The suspect was taken into custody and lowered from the roof in a caged gurney hooked up to a cable.

On this particular day, I was wearing a Class A uniform: wool pants and a long sleeve wool shirt with a black clip-on tie and tie clip. Officer Hankins was also dressed in a Class A uniform. I recall the suspect's last name was Lopez. Upon being hoisted down from the roof with the suspect, Hankins and Poochie were standing by when I walked over to them. The suspect looked up at Hankins and said, "You're the one that shot me!" I looked at Lopez, leaned down toward him, and replied, "It was me. How do you like the way that shit works? You're under arrest for robbery punk!"

Robbery Homicide Division
(Officer Involved Shooting Section)

Whenever you are involved in an officer-involved shooting there is a protocol in place to procure vital and necessary information for responding officers, supervisors, and investigators. It's called a public safety statement and involves a certain procedure. Unfortunately, this was not my first rodeo!

Public Safety Statement

The supervisor receiving the PSS shall state the following to officers substantially involved in a shooting (OIS): "Officer, I am ordering you to give me a public safety statement. Due to the immediate need to take action, you do not have the right to wait for representation to answer these limited questions." The supervisor shall then ask the following questions: 1. Were you involved in an officer-involved shooting? 2. Approximately how many rounds did you fire, and in what direction did you fire them? 3. Do you know if any other officers fired any rounds? 4. Is it possible the suspect fired rounds at you? If so, from what direction were the rounds fired? 5. Is anyone injured? If so, where are they located? 6. Are you aware of any witnesses? If so, what is their location? 7. Approximately where were you when you fired the rounds? 8. Are there any outstanding suspects? If so, what is the description, direction, and mode of travel? How long have they been gone? What crime(s) are they wanted for? What weapons are they armed with? 9. Are there any weapons or evidence that need to be secured/protected? Where are they located?

These questions are followed by the order NOT to discuss the incident with ANYONE, with the exception of legal representation, prior to the arrival of the assigned investigators.

Interview and Walk Through

After providing my PSS, I was transported by to the station to be interviewed. I wanted to let my wife know that I was OK, so I called her and left a message on the home phone. She finally called me hours later after leaving freaking Nordstroms. In any event, it was time to be interviewed regarding what would be my **last** officer-involved shooting as a member of the Los Angeles Police Department.

The assigned detective/investigator from Robbery Homicide Division was Wally Montgomery (RIP). Montgomery and his partner took me through the entire process. I articulated to them that the shooting was an immediate defense of life situation based solely on my knowledge of the suspect, his aggressive actions, and my tactics before, during, and after the shooting. During the course of the investigation, a weapon was recovered from the crime scene.

During my walk through, I recalled briefly speaking with Deputy Chief Gil, who had responded to the scene. I felt confident that my actions were proper, legal, and justified.

Behavioral Science Section

Whenever an officer-involved-shooting with hits occur, officers are ordered to Behavioral Services Section (BSS), to be evaluated by a city of Los Angeles clinical psychologist. The purpose of such an evaluation is to determine if you have any lasting effects from such a traumatic incident, which impacts those involved in different ways. For me, I slept like a baby after the shooting. I remember being scheduled to speak with Dr. Angela Donahue. I was evaluated and cleared to return to full duty, no restrictions. The shooting investigation took several months to be fully investigated, reviewed, and heard before the Use of Force Review Board.

Use of Force Review Board Ruling

(OIS No. 97-14)

The Use of Force Review Board convened to adjudicate my February 21, 1997 officer-involved shooting. As I mentioned earlier, the UOF Review Board looks at several facets when rendering their decision. For instance, what prompted my response, decision-making and judgment, and my tactics before, during, and after the shooting. In addition, they reviewed input and concerns of commanding officers.

Shooting Adjudication

The Board ruled my tactics were appropriate, the drawing of my weapon was ruled in-policy, and, of course, the actual use-of-force was ruled in-policy.

While writing this book, I have contacted several of the officers mentioned. I spoke to retired Sergeant II Mike Beloud, who was a Police Officer III during the officer-involved shooting on February 21, 1997. I told Beloud that I had mentioned him and Fernie in my book regarding my Fiddler on the Roof, officer-involved shooting. Beloud responded with a text message, which I thought was hilarious and worthy of mentioning:

"Maurice Landrum, me n Fernie were talking (and laughing) about this at my retirement party. Make sure to include that it dawned on me that you shot the suspect when your ejected shell casing bounced off the side of my head, actually one hell of a shot from that distance and angle."

CHAPTER 25

Promotion and Retirement

After my officer-involved shooting, I continued to work as a field supervisor at Northeast Patrol Division until October 25, 1998, when I transferred back to Southeast Patrol Division as one of three CRASH gang supervisors. The CRASH Unit's Officer-in-Charge was Sergeant Morris W. Batts, who was 18CR20; I was 18CR30, and Sergeant Pete Zarcone, now Deputy Chief Pete Zarcone, was 18CR40. We had a tall order to fulfill; gang violence was rampant and out of control. There were approximately 24 CRASH officers assigned to the unit, in addition to, two Los Angeles County Probation Officers.

I had several reasons for requesting a transfer back to Southeast Patrol Division. However, the most important reason was to get an opportunity to work as a gang supervisor with one of the Department's well-respected gang supervisors, Morris Batts. He have recruited me for the position and I gladly accepted.

Changing of the guard within Southeast CRASH

Sergeant Batts was subsequently promoted to the position of Sergeant II and transferred into 77th Street Patrol Division. He would eventually become their Divisional Training Coordinator. In the meantime, the Southeast CRASH Unit was assigned as part of Southeast Detectives. Captain Tammy Tatreau was our assigned Commanding Officer. A lieutenant transferred into Southeast Detectives from Internal Affairs Division. There were already two other former Internal Affairs Division supervisors assigned to Southeast Patrol Division as well.

It was obvious this particular lieutenant had been away from patrol operations and really did not have a grasp or clue how the CRASH unit operated. He told the supervisors assigned to CRASH with a straight face, that if we were going to leave the city of Los Angeles on a follow-up, Captain Tatreau had directed us to contact him first!

Well since I was not a climber looking for my next promotion, I wanted to verify the "BS" he was implementing:

Me: "So, just to be clear, sir, you are telling me that if our officers are in fresh pursuit of a shooting suspect during an active crime scene, which leads them into the cities of Gardena, Compton, or wherever, you want us to stop what we are doing and notify you?"

Him: "Yes, that's what the Captain has requested."

That's when I knew CRASH was in trouble. Captain Tatreau had all the confidence in the world in this CRASH unit. What we were dealing with was an insecure lieutenant, who wanted to be relevant. It was painfully obvious that he had worked one to many deployment periods in Internal Affairs. There was a lack of trust and absolutely no transformational leadership. Apparently, he had forgotten that a team was not a group of people who just worked together. A team was a group of people who trusted each other. This statement will make sense in just a few moments!

It was obvious that I made the top of his least-favorite supervisor's list. To top matters off, Captain Tatreau had been transferred out of Southeast Division onto her next assignment. So, Captain I Charlie Beck replaced her. Did I mention Captain Beck had worked the Special Operations Section (SOS), Internal Affairs Group? So, we had IAG South all assigned to Southeast Patrol Division: Rupert, Fontanetta, Katona, and now Beck. Now the shenanigans were about to start!

During this time, I was out sick for a couple of weeks dealing with a gastrointestinal tract infection. So, I filed the employee claim for workers' compensation benefits, and under question 6, it stated, Describe injury and part of body affected. I wrote, "Suffering from gastrointestinal stress." So, I'm off with a righteous medical condition and had been prescribed medications for bacteria in my bloodstream. Sergeant Robert Renstrom was the Southeast IOD Coordinator. In any event, Detective II Charlie Stubbs and Lieutenant Rupert showed up to my home with a gun letter to confiscate my duty weapon.

I immediately invited Stubbs into my home, however, not so much for Rupert. He remained outside. I told Stubbs something wasn't right about what was going on. Charlie concurred; however, he had been ordered to confiscate my duty weapon.

After reviewing the letter, it was obvious that someone had altered and changed my original IOD paperwork. So, I ended up getting a doctor's note from my personal care provider to return to full active duty with no restrictions. When I attempted to return to work, I was advised that I would need to go to Central Receiving to take the Minnesota Multiphasic Personality Inventory (MMPI) psychological test.

The MMPI was given to all LAPD applicants during the hiring process. I knew something was definitely going on for sure now. I spoke to Dr. Staley, the head doctor at Central Receiving, who advised me that anytime someone uses the term "stress," it is handled differently. I explained to him that my situation was a physiological medical condition, not a psychological condition.

When, I showed him my medical paperwork, he agreed with me. Dr. Staley suggested that if I would be willing to release my medical records that would speed up the process to get me returned to full active duty.

During my visit, I vividly recall a Korean officer walking into Central Receiving to get a return to duty. He had been off due to psychological reasons, but received a full return to duty order without any problem. Back then; I heard there was a doctor by the name of Riser, who was the department's go-to person. I believe the plan was to keep me on the rubber gun squad by conducting a fitness for duty evaluation. It would all backfire!

I kept a detailed chronological record of the entire fiasco. I took the MMPI test and met with Clinical Psychologist Dr. Bygot. Our appointment lasted approximately 10 to 15 minutes before she issued me a return to full duty with no restrictions work order. I drove to Southeast Station and handed Lieutenant Ron Katona my return-to-duty work order with no restrictions.

A patrol pilot program called District Policing had been instituted where a lieutenant was assigned as the Officer-in-Charge of Patrol Operations and the Captain I was re-assigned as the Officer-in-Charge of Detective Operations. During this time, Lieutenant Katona was the Patrol CO.

I remember handing him my return-to-full-duty without any restrictions orders and having him open up the office safe so I could retrieve my department-issued .38-caliber revolver. My next stop was to meet with Sergeant Robert Renstrom, the IOD Coordinator, to ask him who had changed my original IOD paperwork to state the body part affected as "mind."

During our conversation, Sergeant Renstrom shared with me that Lieutenants Fontanetta and Rupert were the involved parties. Renstrom changed it back to the body part affected as, "Gastrointestinal Stress." In the meantime, I procured a copy of the paperwork that had been changed without my knowledge or permission. I had been consulting legal counsel.

I went upstairs to change into uniform when, suddenly, in walks Lieutenant Rupert. I knew this was about to become interesting because, to my knowledge, he had never stepped foot into the men's locker room. Rupert displayed a fake smile and stated, "Welcome back! Hey, do you have kids? Do you take them fishing? I have a couple of grandsons maybe we can go fishing sometime." I responded, "We don't fish!" I'm fairly certain that Renstrom or Katona got on the horn to alert him I was in the building.

I can tell you that one of the reasons, if not the main reason, he was attempting to be my new best friend was because he happened to be on the captain's list to be promoted. I'm sure he was worried about me filing a civil lawsuit. I kept wondering what was Fontanetta's story and how he fit into the equation.

Well, it came to me. When I was first assigned to Southeast CRASH, there were several CRASH officers who played football for the department's Centurion football team. During a road trip to Dallas, there was an incident that occurred in a nightclub owned by former Dallas Cowboy, Michael Irving. Later, Internal Affairs Group initiated a massive investigation, and some of the Southeast CRASH officers had been accused of misconduct and needed employee representation for their interviews. So, a couple of the officers asked me if I would sit in and represent them during their interviews. I agreed to sit in for a couple of interviews.

Fontanetta obviously took exception to that. The IA investigators at the time wanted to show individual photographs to the accused officers and get them to identify other involved officers. I advised the IA investigators, they needed to place any single photographs in a photographic six-pack for fairness. It was obvious that I pissed them off. Oh well, don't take short cuts!

There were other violations of AB3300, Peace Officer Procedural Bills of Rights that were being perpetrated. My philosophy was do the right things for the right reasons, which meant being fair, having integrity and avoiding violating officer's rights for the sake of an investigation.

In any investigation, the facts are the facts and the truth will come to light. The majority of investigators assigned to IA during that time were using the position as a stepping-stone to get promoted to the rank of lieutenant. Now don't get me wrong, there were some decent and respectable supervisors assigned to IA. Notice, I used the term: "Some."

So getting back to my return to duty. Captain Beck made a command decision to reassign me from my position as a CRASH supervisor to being assigned to Day Watch Patrol, sitting in as the Acting Watch Commander. During that time, Captain III Richard Bonneau was our Area Commanding Officer. I wanted a valid reason why I was no longer assigned to CRASH. Captain Bonneau and Beck seem to ignore me for the entire deployment period. Finally, I had a meeting with captains Bonneau and Beck in Bonneau's office.

Captain Beck started out with his standard bullshit, "Moe, we're are glad you were able to make it back to work." The primary focus of this meeting for me was to get straightforward answers, like why I had not been allowed to return to my previous assignment as a CRASH Unit supervisor.

Captain Beck replied with more bullshit and said, "We are going in a new direction!" That's when I asked him, "What direction are you going in?" He didn't have an answer. Then, Captain Bonneau opened his lower desk drawer and claimed Captain Tatreau had provided him with a list of concerns. Now keep in mind, there was no allegations of misconduct, just bullshit! I waited, as Bonneau pretended to search his drawer, but wasn't able to produce the list of concerns! I knew this was all a show. I had gotten along fine with Captain Tatreau; she was the one who gave me the position in the first place.

So, I mentioned how I went out on gastrointestinal stress and how Rupert and Fontanetta had altered my IOD paperwork to state that the body part affected was "the mind."

I told Captain Beck, he should strongly consider initiating an independent investigation into the conduct of Rupert and Fontanetta. Once again, he tried to deflect that request with more bullshit by saying, "Moe, we are glad you are back to work."

I was pissed and told Captain Beck in a professional manner verbatim, "Sir, I have little faith in your leadership abilities." Captain Beck responded, "Moe, I wish you didn't feel that way. I responded, "Sir, that's how I feel!" Guess what everyone? I still feel the same way today. Mayor Villaragosa would eventually appoint him to Chief of Police. I had retired in October 2004, way before his appointment. It was nepotism central during his tenure as chief and filled with scandal. The Los Angeles Times sold a lot of newspapers thanks to LAPD upper management.

So here is the million-dollar question: Would you suddenly retire from your position, in the middle of your second term as Chief of Police? Would you just walk away from a yearly salary worth approximately, $349,565.00? Is that normal or do you believe the Mayor of Los Angeles; Eric Garcetti finally had enough of the shenanigans? Judge for yourself!

I know for a fact the majority of hardworking men and women during his tenure, as Chief did not have confidence in his ability to lead the department forward any longer. There was low morale and a clear lack of true leadership and trust, however, there was plenty of nepotism. There were two clearly different standards for discipline.

Captain Beck Out; Captain Nancy Lauer In

Well getting back to my infamous meeting. Captain Beck would eventually be transferred out of Southeast Patrol Division and replaced by Captain Nancy Lauer. The District Policing Pilot Program was still in full effect. So, Lieutenant Regina Scott became the Patrol OIC. I asked Scott for an opportunity to work the Divisional Complaint Unit. Since Sergeant Henry Quan had been recently promoted to the position of Assistant Watch Commander, there was a vacancy.

The following deployment period, I would be assigned to the Divisional Complaint Unit. I knew if I wanted to be promoted again, I had to have completed staff work experience. Being assigned to the Divisional Complaint Unit would fulfill that requirement. When I started, the unit consisted of Detective Gary McQueen, Detective Wayne Bootow, Sergeants Ietia Eston, and Ted Malliet (RIP). Within a couple of deployment periods, I was selected as the OIC of the Complaint Unit.

I spent the next year there until the lieutenants were rotated around again. By this time, a new lieutenant had been assigned as the OIC of Patrol. I was very familiar with him and we never saw eye-to-eye.

It all started when he was a Sergeant at Southwest Patrol Division and I was a Police Officer III. He had written this two-page Sergeant's log entry, which I refused to sign. His log entry alleged that I had <u>purposely drove through a crime scene</u> on Exposition Place near 2nd Avenue. That morning, I waited for Captain Deal, our Patrol Commanding Officer at the time. I responded to his worthless log entry and wrote a response on a Form 15.7, which I personally hand, delivered to Captain Deal. His log entry was full of nonsense was squashed and no further action would be taken.

So, here we are years later, he is now my immediate supervisor. Back then; everyone assigned to the Complaint Unit, with the exception of me, had attended the three-day IA School. I wanted to attend this particular school to have it for my resume. I made a couple of phone calls and reached out to the IA Training Coordinator, who disclosed that he would hold the last open spot for me pending the approval of my direct supervisor. I spoke to Sergeant II Cathy Meeks, our Divisional Training Coordinator, and she directed me to my immediate supervisor.

I walked into his office, and before I could complete my sentence, he responded, "No." I looked at him and responded, "Why?" He responded, "The answer is No, you not going to attend the course." I responded, "You know, I have been assigned to the Complaint Unit for approximately one year. I think it's time for me to be rotated back into patrol next deployment period or as soon as possible."

LEADERSHIP 101: As a leader can you truthfully answer this question: Do those you lead like, respect, and trust you? If your subordinates are only respecting you solely based on your rank, you need to re-evaluate the art of leadership. Remember Ethics, Integrity, and Loyalty make up a real leader, not Fear, Ignorance, and Intimidation based on your rank.

You see, true leadership is a reciprocal relationship between those who lead and those who decide to follow. In this true-life scenario, I was not about to follow him anywhere. Simply put, he had no leadership skills—rank, yes; leadership skills, no! Every true leader understands that trust is achieved only when a leader earns and maintains credibility with all diverse groups within the department. Based on my experience, he truly lacked the ability to maintain an environment that enabled all employees to develop, flourish, and contribute their full potential toward the department's mission, goals, and core values! Real talk! He seemed to have a problem with certain ethnic groups, I'm just saying!

By the next deployment period, I was assigned to Morning Watch. I'm pretty sure, in his mind, he thought he had screwed me. But, I was working the watch that I wanted to work. You see, as a field supervisor, you have to be proficient in four distinct areas: field tactics, complaint investigations, vehicle pursuits and use-of-force investigations. I was proficient in all these areas and looked forward to being a Field Supervisor once again. One morning, at end of watch, I walked into the Complaint Office to use an available computer to complete my sergeant's log. The other computers in the sergeant's room were all occupied.

When I left, Bootow informed me that the same lieutenant, who just couldn't help himself, had told him and Malliet that I did not belong in their office, in addition to some other inappropriate things about me. Well, what he didn't count on was they both had my back and told me what was said. Bootow also told me to list him as a witness. I reduced to writing the lieutenant's improper remarks via 15.7 correspondence and addressed it to Captain Bonneau.

Karma is such a beautiful thing. A couple of deployment periods later, I arrive for my Morning Watch shift. The Watch Commander advised me that Captain Lauer wanted me to drive her around the city during my tour of duty. She had been designated as the on-duty Command Duty Officer (CDO). As, I rode around with Captain Lauer; we discussed my hostile work environment complaint filed against the lieutenant. I recalled Captain Lauer saying, "You know sometimes Moe, you could win the battle, but not the war." Then, out of nowhere, she asked me to be her Patrol Adjutant.

I looked at her and asked for permission to speak freely. She responded, "Go ahead." I stated, "Ma'am, I don't think it would be a good idea for me to be the Patrol Adjutant. I have a real problem with the lieutenant's lack of diversity, fairness, and understanding." She responded by saying that problem had been resolved. I was like, what do you mean, "resolved?" She said, "Well, starting next deployment period, patrol operations will be going back to the way it used to be with the Captain I taking back over Patrol Operations. You would be working for me."

Patrol Adjutant

What a beautiful thing. He was out and back on Morning Watch and life was good. I remember he would write these long watch commanders log entries, making all sorts of ridiculous recommendations for the Captain to consider. What was cool, she would ask for my input on some of the absurdity he had written. A lot of his so-called ideas were file in the nearest trash bin.

Everyone knew he had a sponsor who would eventually retire and go on to become the Chief of Police at another local police department. The lieutenant would eventually be promoted to the rank of Captain and finished his career as the commanding officer of Communications Division, which is apparently where the department assigns you when they want to keep you away from a Patrol Divisions, "Kind of like out of sight, out of mind!" If has a familiar theme, there was another Captain that ended his career there as well.

FINAL CHAPTER

While serving as the Patrol Adjutant at Southeast Patrol Division, I had received a call from Captain Bob Green, the Officer-in-Charge during the time of a joint LAPD/FBI Gang Taskforce. They were conducting a Racketeer Influenced and Corrupt Organizations (RICO) Act investigation on a local Blood street gang from Southwest Patrol Division. As a gang expert for that particular gang, he wanted me to provide their detail with some gang intelligence.

So, basically, they wanted information about some of the gang members who were the focus of the RICO investigation. The taskforce was housed within the South Traffic and former D.A.R.E. offices located at 4125 South Crenshaw Boulevard, Los Angeles (Southwest Patrol Division jurisdiction). I drove there and provided the requested information.

Promotion to Sergeant II

Upon leaving the taskforce's offices and walking through the common hallway of South Traffic Division, I spoke to the Commanding Officer of South Traffic Division (STD). I said, "Excuse me, ma'am. I noticed South Traffic Division had advertised for a Sergeant II (Assistant Watch Commander) position, but the open application filing date has expired." She told me that if I was interested I should submit my application before my end of watch. I drove back to Southeast Station, filled out the appropriate paperwork, and dropped it off on my way home.

Several weeks later, I was interviewed for the position. After the interview, I did not hear anything for a couple of weeks. Early one Monday morning while at work, I received a telephone call from the Captain of STD, who advised me that she was going to elevate me to the rank and position of Sergeant II. That was great news, especially since Captain III Jim Miller, the Commanding Officer of 77th Street Patrol Division, had told me that I would never be promoted to the rank of Sergeant II because of my involvement at 39th Street and Dalton Avenue, even though I had been promoted twice after the incident. Of course, I filed a grievance against Captain Miller and won. Thank you, sir, for motivation to prove you wrong!

I was invited to attend South Traffic Division's deployment meeting, where the Captain introduced me to the other supervisors and staff. In the meantime, Captain Lauer was happy for me, but I would not be able to transfer until I trained my replacement. So, I actually wrote a quick reference book titled, "*Patrol Adjutant, aka Panic Room.*" I trained my replacement and transferred to the new assignment by the end of my deployment period. I am forever grateful for the opportunity that Captain Lauer gave me, which no doubt helped me to be promoted.

South Traffic Division

Now, it was time to face a new challenge. I had 20.5 years of service on the job and had never been assigned to any traffic division. However, I had handled my share of traffic collision investigations throughout my career. I recall during my first week the Captain called me into her office and asked me if I would mind sitting in as her Adjutant while her secretary, Melinda, went on vacation. What do you say to the person that promoted you? I responded, "No, ma'am, I don't mind!" She even threw me a bone and gave me weekends off. There were other issues going on within South Traffic Division. The Training Coordinator was out on leave due to some sort of hostile work environment situation.

So, I also became the temporary Training Coordinator as well. The Captain had a 100% project submittal, which meant any projects assigned to South Traffic Division by Operations South Bureau were turned in on time. This perfect project rating came at a cost to her subordinates. The officers and civilian staff were a great bunch of professionals. She lived and breathed South Traffic Division. I never met anyone, let alone a Commanding Officer, who would arrive to work by 0800 hours and would not go end of watch until 6 or 6:30 p.m. There were times when she would arrive at her residence, which was five to ten minutes away, and then call me at the station to inquire if there was anything happening that impacted her command at South Traffic Division.

It got to the point that I had to tell her, "Ma'am, if anything occurs that requires notifications to be made, I can assure that you will be the first person notified, followed by Operations South Bureau and the Department's Command Post." I appreciated my time working South Traffic Division. As I mentioned, I had the opportunity to work with some awesome supervisors, officers, and civilian staff members.

Death of my Father

While assigned to South Traffic Division, my father, Maurice Leo Landrum Sr., a United States Marine who fought in the Korean Conflict, died on Monday, October 27, 2003. I had taken off work per the Family Medical Leave Act for approximately two weeks prior to his death. At approximately 0300 hours that day, I was due back to work. Fontana Citrus Nursing Home called and informed me that my father had transitioned. I remember notifying the Captain. I was devastated. My hero, my father, and the person who dropped me off and picked me up from the Los Angeles Police Academy for approximately five months was gone onto Glory.

I recalled completing his obituary, making the appropriate notifications, and planning his funeral service all before noon that day. My father had received an honorable discharge from the United States Marine Corps and would be laid to rest at the Riverside National Cemetery.

Act of Kindness

I will forever be grateful for one particular special act of kindness. On the day of my father's funeral, my family and I had arrived at the church for my father's home going service. The Captain had phoned me and asked if it would be OK, if she sent a couple of motor officers to escort my father's mortuary transport vehicle during the funeral procession.

Prior to receiving that call, I was in the process of paying for a couple of funeral escorts. On the morning of my father's home going service, my family and I arrived at the church via the family car. Upon exiting the car, I observed LAPD Motor Sergeant Charles Johnson along with six uniformed motor officers from South Traffic Division. I walked up to Johnson, choking back tears, to thank him and the officers for their support and presence. Johnson replied, "Moe, this is what we do. We take care of our own brother!"

I have always been proud to be a member of the Los Angeles Police Department. This act of kindness was just one of the many reasons. During the funeral procession, I just stared out of the passenger window thinking to myself, "Dad you are the man! Being escorted by some of the finest police officers in the world.

You get to run every red light and stop sign. My sons, nephews and two of my former partners, Morris W. Batts and Johnnie Jones, were honorary pallbearers that day. Semper Fi, Dad!

San Bernardino County Employment

One early Monday morning in August 2004, I decided to check the County of San Bernardino Human Resources website for employment opportunities. I noted the County of San Bernardino, Office of the District Attorney, Bureau of Investigation had announced they were hiring. I decided to submit an application just for the hell of it. After about three weeks, I received a telephone call from the Chief Investigator's Executive Secretary. She informed me that based on my education and work experience; I would be eligible for the position of Senior District Attorney Investigator, as opposed to District Attorney Investigator.

She scheduled me for an oral interview, which consisted of a three-member panel of Supervisor Investigators: Ransdale, Thompson, and Janbonski. During my interview, I was asked, what did I know about real estate fraud? I informed the panel that I did not know anything about real estate fraud but that I had a grant deed and deed of trust recorded on my home and that I could investigate anything. During the interview, Supervisor Janbonski informed me that he was a retired Sergeant from the Los Angeles Police Department. Upon completing the interview, I was advised they only had one position open and if I made it to the Chief's oral, I would be notified. Later that afternoon, I received a telephone call from Chief Mike Smith's Executive Secretary, who informed me about the Chief's Oral. She scheduled me, and I appeared before Assistant Chiefs Mike Donovan and Richard Hendricksen.

At the conclusion of that interview, Donovan told me that they would be meeting with the Chief to make a decision within the next couple of days. I received a telephone call later that afternoon from Donovan, who gave me a conditional job offer pending a law enforcement pre-employment background check, polygraph, drug test, and medical examination. Within three weeks after the conditional job offer, I was hired as a Senior District Attorney Investigator.

Closing Thoughts

I have had an interesting law enforcement career as a member of the Los Angeles Police Department. I saw more than the average police officer will ever see during their tenure. In the early eighties, life as a Los Angeles police officer was challenging, dangerous, and interesting. I want to personally thank the many people who I had an opportunity to work with during my tenure with the Los Angeles Police Department. For those, who attempted to destroy me, it only made me stronger. At the end of the day, I kept God in my corner!

Matthew 7:7 "Ask and it will be given to you; seek and you will find; knock and the door will be opened to you. For everyone who asks receives;

the one who seeks finds; and to the one who knocks, the door will be opened."

On October 2, 2004, after 21.5 years of dedicated service, I retired honorably from the Los Angeles Police Department. As I reflect back over my career, I had one hell of a ride. The capers discussed in this book are all true. I have dozens and dozens of capers that occurred during my tenure as a Los Angeles Police Officer. This book was written to share just a portion of them with family, friends and those readers curious about what street life and career survival were really like for me as a police officer. I never openly discussed my experience as a Los Angeles Police Officer with my loved ones. Around my family, I was like a teddy bear. At work, while in uniform, locked and loaded, I was your nightmare if you WERE a suspect, who preyed upon innocent victims.

"In my heart and mind, I believe there is no greater honor bestowed upon me or any member of the Los Angeles Police Department than to truly protect and serve those who call upon us to restore a sense of calm, safety, and normalcy within their communities."

~Maurice L. Landrum Jr.~

Special Thanks

I would like to acknowledge Mrs. Stephanie Graham for her editorial suggestions and assistance along the way! Thank you for helping me bring my true tale of street life and career survival as a member of the Los Angeles Police Department to life!

REFERENCES

1. CDCR.CA.Gov – Inmate Locator (Public Access)

2. Mitchell, J. L. (2001, March 14). The Raid That Still Haunts L.A. *Los Angeles Times*

3. Serrano, R. (1990, December 6). Session Before Dalton Raid Described. *Los Angeles Times,*

4. *Los Angeles Times,* June 20, 1991 (New Article) 3 Officers Acquitted in 39th-Dalton Drug Raid: Trial: Jurors say they believe vandalism

5. *Los Angeles Times,* June 23, 2012 (New Article) South L.A. serial killer gets death sentence

6. Website: lapdonline.org-Basic Area Map of Harbor, Pacific, Southwest, Northeast, and Southeast